I SEE DEAD CHURCHES

A.T. Hargrave

I SEE DEAD CHURCHES

& THEIR COMING RESURRECTION

TATE PUBLISHING & Enterprises

Published by Tate Publishing & Enterprises, LLC
127 E. Trade Center Terrace | Mustang, Oklahoma 73064 USA
1.888.361.9473 | www.tatepublishing.com

Tate Publishing is committed to excellence in the publishing industry. The company reflects the philosophy established by the founders, based on Psalm 68:11,
"The Lord gave the word and great was the company of those who published it."

Book design copyright © 2010 by Tate Publishing, LLC. All rights reserved.
Cover design by Amber Gulilat
Interior design by Stephanie Woloszyn

Published in the United States of America

ISBN: 978-1-61663-743-9
1. Religion / Christian Church / General   2. Religion / Christian Life / General
10.08.11

DEDICATION

I dedicate this book to all those dreamers who knew there had to be more to Christianity and church life and sacrificed to experience it. Your faith has been contagious!

ACKNOWLEDGMENTS

Mom and Dad, thank you for loving Jesus in front of me. Thank you for actually believing that I could do anything. You believed in me when I didn't and embraced sacrifice when I wouldn't. I owe you more than I could ever repay. Crestwood, thanks for being patient and giving me room to grow. You have endured the difficult, are embracing the impossible, and your future is beautiful. You are a beautiful people with a big destiny. To my wife, Micki, you are the clearest reflection of Jesus to me. Thank you!

TABLE OF CONTENTS

FOREWORD

by Jim Hylton
Fort Worth, Texas

The heart of God is exposed in the writings of A.T. Hargrave. Reflections of God's heart come from a life fully committed to Him, study with a goal to know Him, and experience gained with Him. He grew up in a climate of faith with his pastor father and godly mother. His most formative years were spent in a church open to the Holy Spirit's guidance. A major influence in his life was Dr. Brad Jones, pastor of Crestwood Baptist Church in Oklahoma City, Oklahoma. He was a man full of the Holy Spirit, full of faith and full of vision. At the center of his vision was the Lord Jesus who gave him the vision of reaching and training people at home and around the world. Crestwood Baptist Church was and is a place where Jesus is welcome to be Himself. In that nurturing climate A.T. Hargrave grew as a young associate pastor. When the Lord called Brad Jones home, A.T. became one of the leaders and now serves as their senior pastor.

This book is alive with reality, the reality of the Lord. Insights that can only come from the Lord and from personal experience fill the pages. You will be guided where Jesus was guided—to know and spend time with the Father. The Father's love, the Father's provisions, the Father's power, and the Father's plans for you will speak to your heart. This is a well-written book. But better still, it is a well-lived book. It has been field tested in the life of A.T. Hargrave. A.T. lives it, and so can you. Receive it, embrace the insights found herein, and pass these insights on to others.

God's heart, found clearly in these writings, gives insight into the kingdom's operations, church life that expresses His body, and God's will being done as it is in heaven. These insights will relate to the beginner on the journey or the most mature person. Both beginners and those already equipped will be challenged.

Enjoy this book and make other's aware of it. Give it or loan your copy so that the refreshing that comes from the presence of the Lord will be enjoyed by countless others.

It is my privilege to share with you the presentation of this book. In 1997, a prophetic word was given to me. A part of that word was that my descendants would go further in serving the Lord than I have. That is a very sobering word. Two questions come to mind: how far have I set the standard, and how much further will my descendants go? This book, written by my son, is an indication of that prophetic word.

He believes, as I do, that revival is and always has been more than a moment in time, it is a culture to live in. The apostle Paul tells us that it is God's desire to dwell with us and be active among us (2 Corinthians 6:16). The church today has created a lot of substitutions for God's presence and activity. It is an adult version of "playing church." We are all guilty of that, but here is the good news, the promise still stands! He still wants to be your God, and you his child. He still longs for you to know His presence and witness His activity. A.T. shares just how to do that in this brief, yet deep word to you. Join him in learning who you are in the heart of God and how much of Him He (the Father) is wanting you to know and experience. Come to live in revival: receive His grace by faith, rest in His grace by faith, rejoice in His grace by faith, and reveal His grace through your faith.

Until His work is completed in us,

—Tom Hargrave,
pastor of Wards Chapel Baptist Church
Atoka, Oklahoma

INTRODUCTION:
DRINK OR SWIM

Revival, renewal, and reformation are the talk of the Christian community. Many are praying for them, some are fighting against them, and others are trying to figure out what they are. There are numerous books and a variety of tapes and CDs promising to provide people with a revival experience. But what if God is not simply looking to give an experience of revival but to create a culture to host it? Could we be praying for revival while He is looking for someone to carry it? Could we be asking for a drink when He wants us to swim?

I believe He is looking for a people to host His glorious, beautiful, powerful presence. It is my heart's desire to become one of those people and raise up a generation full of individuals who can host His presence—carry revival—to shape the culture and, inevitably, our future. Many Christians and churches have been playing small-ball thinking they are being "humble," all the while missing out on their Father's passion. It is my conviction that Father God is looking for sons and daughters who are prepared to make life adjustments to host His manifest presence.

Jesus, speaking of the kingdom of God, told these two parables:

> Again, the kingdom of heaven is like a treasure hidden in a field, which a man found and hid; and for joy over it he goes and sells all that he has and buys that field. Again, the kingdom of heaven is like a merchant seeking beautiful pearls, who, when he had found one pearl of great price, went and sold all that he had and bought it.
>
> Matthew 13:44–46

Revival, renewal, and reformation are simply expressions of the kingdom of God. Notice in the first parable that the kingdom is the "treasure." I believe this refers to how we ought to view the kingdom. The kingdom is worth gladly selling all that we have to obtain it. However, the next example says the kingdom is like the "merchant," not the pearl. I believe we are the pearl. God gave up His son—His everything—for us, the "pearl of great price."

My point is that the group of people in which God wants to host His presence will be a people who value the kingdom the way God has valued His people—a people who enjoy grace the way the Father enjoyed giving it, a people who are as passionate about the kingdom as the King is about His people.

The following pages contain truths that I believe are needed for us to be cultivated into this kind of people. I pray that these truths will become revelation by the Holy Spirit and seep down past the intellect of your mind and into your heart, where I am confident they will change you!

part 1

WHAT IS KILLING OUR CHURCHES?

HIS BEAUTIFUL BRIDE

I love the local church. I pastor a small, traditional, inner-city church and love it. I grew up in a small, rural, traditional church in the little town of Atoka, Oklahoma. I do not pastor a mega-church or have outstanding credentials. Matter of fact, as I am writing this, my church has closed down a portion of its facility while we raise money to fix the heating. I am not the guy I would have picked to write this, but what I have seen has forever changed me. I have seen a dead church experience renewal. I have had the privilege of pastoring a group of people who are going through the difficult, who are embracing the impossible, and who are experiencing the supernatural. The Lord has used this special group to teach me that He is not finished yet. I am simply a homegrown boy who loves Jesus and His bride, the church, and who believes we are on the verge of something big!

I do not wish to be a catalyst for hopelessness or to be a preacher of doom. Actually, my intention is the opposite. I wish to point out both the obvious decline in the church and what I believe to be His solution for it. Jesus's bride is beautiful and her future is also!

I haven't always felt this way. I am a part of a group some have labeled "postmodern." I used to hold to a theology that allowed me to think I was in love with Jesus while hating the object of His affections: His church. As I have come to know Him better, I have begun to see how crazy, head-over-heels in love with her He really is. This does not mean that He agrees with everything she has done; it simply points out how great and unconditional His love really is.

A Sobering Thought

Recently I read an article about the coming evangelical collapse. The article was strictly fact-driven, but the facts were enough to break just about anyone's denial of the present fallout in the evangelical community. The statistics were staggering: memberships have declined, salvations have declined, and baptisms have declined. It appears that if we continue as we are, we will cease to exist in only a couple of generations. The statistics were for all traditional denominations (i.e. Baptist, Methodist, Presbyterian, Lutheran, etc.). Our money is running out, our enthusiasm is depleting, and our outreach is becoming ineffective.

Our seniors are passing on while we are doing a less-than-okay job of reaching the younger generations. We have offered quick fixes by developing advanced youth ministries that teach students how to be entertained, while never actually providing them with what will satisfy their hearts (I made that mistake myself in youth ministry). Anytime the main attraction at church is not God Himself, we should stop and reconsider our actions. There are thousands of churches across America that were built to hold hundreds, but now are home to mere handfuls—beautiful, lifeless edifices. Stained glass windows and wooden pews furnished and built by men and women that were planning on being here awhile, but now many of those pews are empty and the stained glass never seen.

Some chalk this up as "a sign of the times," implying that the closer we come to the second coming of Christ for His glorious and conquering bride, the more she becomes defeated and ineffective! So, is it a good thing that we are not overcoming, not affecting our cities? That seems a bit skewed. If a person actually believed that theory, then he could quit witnessing, quit tithing, quit praying for the lost, and therefore speed up Jesus's second coming.

Just recently, the president of my particular denomination wrote an article in which he commented about the need for change to insure our future. It appears that the collapse has already begun, but do not underestimate God. I believe that the greatest move of God on planet earth is about to happen. I also believe that God will not leave out any part of His bride. Do not think for a moment that God is going to bring a worldwide movement of His Spirit and not invite and include the "traditional" part of His bride. Deep down, I believe this great movement of God will start with a divine visitation to the traditional evangelical community. I believe it will be a grassroots reformation starting with pastors and local churches and move across the globe, much like the church's beginning. However, this movement of God will not look the way some evangelicals might think or want, and will not come without some repentance.

Understanding the Seasons

Jesus called the Pharisees hypocrites because they did not understand the season they were in. Hypocrites? Wouldn't they be hypocrites only if they *said* they understood the season but really did not (which I do not believe to be the case)? I believe Jesus called them hypocrites because they claimed to walk with God but did not know the seasons in which they lived. If they knew God, they would have recognized what He was doing on earth. They would have embraced Jesus, not killed Him. Jesus pointed this out, "But you do not have His Word abiding in you, because whom He sent, Him you do not believe." (John 5:38) In Hargrave paraphrase it would be stated, "You do not have God's Word as your core, because when He did something new—sent Me—you did not recognize Me. Because if you had recognized Me, you would have believed."

We must understand that our dilemma is not going to be resolved by building new facilities, or by better publicity, or even by worship style changes—even though those things are fine and, in some cases, needed. For the past decade or so, a saying among emergent church leaders has been, "We can change the method without changing the message." But the method is not the only reason we are in this present position. What if the message we are presenting is incomplete? What if the Scriptures point out something more and we keep teaching our usual message, while God wants to build on that message? The writer of Hebrews mentions, "leaving the discussion of the elementary principles of Christ, let us go on to perfection" (Hebrews 6:1). Instead of moving on to perfection, we have huddled around certain truths (denominations) and made them our central theme to keep the focus on elementary principles. Many of us read the verse as saying, "Camping on the elementary principles of Christ, let us stay here where we are comfortable and never go forward." We are not called to camp but to go on to maturity.

Quitters, Campers, and Climbers

I would like to present to you three types of believers, which I believe make up the local church.

First is the *quitter*. A quitter's core problem is a faulty belief system. Whether it was taught from a pulpit or learned by observation, the quitter's belief system is dangerous and often contagious. A quitter will believe that life is supposed to be fair and easy; he will intentionally avoid conflict, ignore pressure situations, and resist change. A quitter will believe that life is a big lottery and will base life on luck or chance instead of on a firm belief in an ever-present God. He believes life is to be accepted, not altered. This will produce an attitude that everything that happens simply happens. Quitters make statements like, "What can I possibly do about it?"

in a surrendered tone. A quitter will carry a victim's mentality. It does not matter what happens—quitters don't see themselves as the problem, but as victims.

Campers are an interesting bunch, because they have begun to climb, but just a little. They will talk about their previous climbs, and even in some cases appear to still be climbing. But be aware this group is not always as it appears. Campers camp. They will retire—not from work—but from facing adversity and taking risks. Campers stop climbing to protect where they are. They protect where they are by arguing "truth," but really it is fear expressing itself in man's wisdom.

For example, a camper will cover up his fear of leaving his comfortable campground with a false wisdom that says, "We do not need to do that; it will cause division." The camper uses false unity to guard his false comfort. Campers will set a goal and, once it is reached, will never go higher. They value comfort more than climbing. Most campers I have met are jealous and critical of climbers (the third type of believer), much like Saul was of David. They cannot stand someone going higher because it reminds them of their complacency—excuse me, their camping. Campers have this habit of comparing themselves to family and peers instead of Jesus. While a climber looks at his own potential, a camper looks at other people.

A *climber* is the only mindset for a Christian to have. The first two mindsets will only leave a Christian unsatisfied, because deep in their DNA is the need to climb. Let me ask you a question that I have asked myself: if everyone in your church had your same devotion to God, where would the church be in ten years? Climbers look at problems and see promises. They see adversity as an invitation to promotion, much like David viewed Goliath. One of the most fundamental characteristics of a climber is the possession of an enduring faith in something bigger than himself. This characteristic is invaluable. I have men in my church who have this quality, which enables them to believe that God is always doing something big and that we are privileged to be a part of it. This attitude creates an environment that is concentrated toward being significant without ever becoming arrogant. We are simply a part of the "big" that God is doing.

Next, a climber accepts responsibility. One of the problems the church has is that mysterious group of people called "they." People would say to me, "We have never done that because 'they' would not let us," or, "You know that 'they' won't like this." Finally, in a meeting with our church leadership, I told them, "We are the 'they.' It is on our watch now; we will take full responsibility for what does or does not happen."

A quitter simply lets life happen (what's the point in fighting it?), campers will blame someone else, but climbers will take responsibility. With this being true, climbers also can take correction. If a climber cannot be an example of how to live, then he will be an example of how to repent. Because a climber is focused on advancing, constructive correction is welcomed. If my focus is on camping, for example, then I will most likely be defensive and call my defensiveness protection.

Climbers have a unique perspective on life. They view life as a race—not against others, but against time. Their question is, "How much can be done before I go home?" instead of the quitter's question, "How long before I go home?" or the camper's, "How can I guard what I have to make sure nothing happens to it until I go home?" This perspective makes a climber constantly desire to know God more, to taste and see more of the kingdom now, before God calls him home. A climber lives out of passion for God and welcomes discipline. A climber sees discipline as creating freedom, not taking it away. Lastly, a climber will invest his money and time in growing the kingdom and himself spiritually.

Which one are you? God has called you and placed inside of you the potential to be a climber. A person can smother that potential through years of camping, but if he can recognize the unsatisfied longing of his heart, the Holy Spirit will guide him back to being a climber. "Friend, go up higher" (Luke 14:10).

GUARD OR GUIDE

Years ago, I heard a story. In a cold, New York winter, a poor man was found dead in an apartment flat. The only things that filled his apartment were stacks and stacks of newspapers he had collected. The city buried him in an unmarked grave, and the only thing left to do was clean out the apartment. As city workers were carrying down stacks of newspapers, one man tripped and lost hold of his bundle of papers, revealing that pressed between every page of every newspaper were dollar bills. I do not remember the exact amount, but it added up to be hundreds of thousands of dollars. That man died of starvation and exposure to the elements, while at his fingertips, pressed between the pages of newspapers, was the resource available to live a life of abundance.

Much like that man, many churches are dying of starvation and exposure, while pressed between the pages of their Bibles is the resource needed to live a life of abundance. Whether in ignorance or arrogance, the resource is not being provided to the people, and it is time to brush the dust off and discover (or rediscover) the one resource that is needed: the kingdom of God. The resource or enabling agent that will empower us to be all that we are called to be, and do what we are called to do, has been right in front of us. The traditional part of the western church is dying while this precious commodity is so close.

The King and His Kingdom

Jesus mentions the kingdom of God or kingdom of heaven over one hundred times in the four gospels. He mentions the church three times (Matthew 16 and 18), and being born again once (John 3). When God inspired men to write the accounts of Jesus, they recorded more of His teachings on the kingdom than on church or even salvation. The Bible says He went throughout all of Galilee preaching the gospel of the kingdom (Matthew 4:23; Mark 1:14; Luke 4:43), if that gives an idea of what was important to Him. His first sermon was "repent for the kingdom of heaven is at hand," (Matthew 4:17) and His last moments with the disciples before He ascended were spent discussing the kingdom of God (Acts 1:3). Jesus does not ever mention a gospel of salvation, but does mention the gospel of the kingdom (Matthew 9:35; Mark 1:14).

The most common topic of Jesus is not the cross or salvation, but the kingdom. In an overview of all four gospels, the Holy Spirit chose to record and focus on the kingdom more than the church or salvation, but in the traditional western church we do the opposite by focusing on salvations and the church. We are commanded to seek the kingdom first (Matthew 6:33), we are told that it pleases God to give the kingdom to us (Luke 12:32), we are taught to pray for the kingdom to come (Luke 11:2), and we are told that the church is given the keys to the kingdom (Matthew 16:). However, many evangelicals do not know what the kingdom is. We have reduced the gospel down to a born-again experience, consequently missing the point: the kingdom.

Do not misunderstand me—salvation is imperative. However, it is the entrance into the kingdom. Matter of fact, if we as a church would seek first the kingdom, we would see more people saved! Jesus told Nicodemus, "Unless one is born again, he cannot see the kingdom of God" (John 3:3). For some this verse means that unless you are saved you will not see heaven in the afterlife. However, Jesus is saying that being born again gives us the ability to see the kingdom now. Jesus said that the kingdom is "at hand." This means that it is reachable. Not distant and "out there," but here. In Luke 17:21, Jesus says, "The kingdom of God is within you." In Luke 19:11–27, Jesus teaches on the kingdom of God and about stewardship, implying that we are to steward the kingdom of God.

The Prison Guard

Paul the apostle gives many different analogies of the law. One that has become tremendously influential is used in his letter to the Galatians. "But before faith came, we were kept under guard by the law, kept for the faith which would afterward be revealed" (Galatians 3:23). The law was a guard. It was designed to keep people in the prison. The next verse describes the law as a tutor; however, that is not an accurate translation of the Greek word *paidagogos*. The word *tutor* or *schoolmaster* would be the translation of the word *didaskalos*. This word used in verse 24 as "tutor" was used by the Greek and Roman families as a title for a slave that was put in charge of guarding the owner's son as he traveled to and from school (Wuest). This is why Paul follows in chapter 4 by saying that a son, though he is heir, does not differ from a slave. Why? Because he is still under the guardianship of the slave.

The law was to administer condemnation. The law put Israel (and us) in a prison based on obedience or disobedience and then stood guard. The law was not intended to express God's attitude towards man. God's attitude is one of grace. Law requires but grace enables. The law was to guard us until Jesus came to blow a hole (salvation) in the side of the prison so we would all flock to "the way" out. Jesus was the way out from under the law. In John 16:13 Jesus shares, "when He, the Spirit of truth, has come, He will guide you into all truth." In the New Testament, after Jesus has made the way out (salvation) and you are out of the prison, there is a great, beautiful, open place called the kingdom. And to make sure we arrive at our destiny, we were given a guide.

Freed from Prison

God made a covenant with Israel. The law was mandated by God as Israel's part of the covenant. But no human could keep the law. God, in His wisdom and deep desire for mercy, instituted the sacrifice—allowing one life to be given for the sins of another. God then did something that no one saw coming: He came to our side of the covenant as a man.

Jesus was circumcised on his eighth day (Luke 2:21). The circumcision was a sign of the covenant. This means that Jesus entered into covenant with God as a man and on the behalf of man. Jesus then kept all the law, being blameless. Now, when we have faith in Christ we become, according to the book of Romans, in Christ. When we are in Christ we keep the law through Christ.

The law judges in terms of obedience or disobedience, whereas the promises of God are measured by faith. A person does not go to hell because they broke the law, but because they did not embrace Jesus Christ by faith. In the Old Testament, the people lived by the law. In the New Testament, they lived by faith. Faith in Christ frees us from the law. The Bible teaches that faith alone places us in relationship with God, and as we grow in intimacy with God, we begin to love God back. So faith in Christ Jesus as my only hope of pleasing the Father is what is solely needed for me to be free from the prison. Jesus has provided all that is needed to escape the prison and follow the guide. However, many Christians have chosen to stay in the prison.

There are only two ways to relate to God: the old covenant way or the new covenant way, to have a guard or a guide. It cannot be both: "But if you are led (guided) by the Spirit, you are not under the law (guarded)" (Galatians 5:18). Many campers have camped just outside the exit that Jesus made in the prison and have not been guided out by the Spirit.

A door is both an exit point and an entry point. If you go out my office door you will, in one step, exit my office and enter our conference room. If you were to return to my office, in one step, you would exit the conference room and enter my office. Jesus is the door out of the prison and into the kingdom. In one step we move from prisoners to princes. That is the redeeming power of God.

The Problem with the Prison

When we choose to remain at the prison and we embrace a culture that believes the church is designated as the guard, death will soon follow. The problem with camping at the prison is three-fold: the law only leads to death, the law will always bring bondage, and we never reach our full potential under the law. The cross made it possible to live free from the law, but many are still choosing to relate to God in a law mentality.

Abundant life only flows from being connected to God. The law can never bring life or righteousness. Many churches have camped out in the prison and, as a result, have become lifeless, because life will never come from the law. The nature of the law is to require obedience, and thus demands death when disobeyed, for the wages of sin is death. The law is not evil; it simply is not enough to bring life. Sin brings death, and we would not have known sin except through the law (Romans 7:7). The law made my awareness of sin increase, resulting in my awareness of death. Because of humanity's inability to keep the law, the law consistently brought death to those who lived by it.

When we choose to remain at the prison, we are choosing death. This is one reason the classical traditions of the Western church is dying. When we choose the law, we are by default choosing to not have relationship with God, therefore, our intimacy with Him suffers. When we preach, teach, and promote that God is in relationship with us based on our performance (obedience), we are in fact promoting the prison and functioning as a guard. This teaching will not bring life to the church.

In the new covenant, God does not enter relationships with us based on our performance; He enters relationships based on His promises. When a person responds to Jesus by faith, apart from any works (performance), God enters a relationship with that person. That person becomes born-again, resulting in a new nature (2 Corinthians 5:17). This new nature does not want to walk in rebellion to God, but wants to please Him. God then enters relationship with people apart from their works and, in doing so, brings life to them, empowering them to live a righteous life. A. W. Tozer sums it up well, "One of the most horrible and wicked lies ever told to man is that after he is saved, he no longer needs to seek God."

The second problem with the law is it always leads to bondage. I need God to enable me to walk upright before Him. However, many teach God will not have relationship with me unless I "act right." Well, if I need God in my life for me to act right but cannot be in relationship with Him without acting right, I am in bondage. I can never arrive where I need to be! We breed frustration into many Christians' walks by a backward teaching of grace. This frustration will inevitably turn into anger and will cause many to give up on the church and God, weakening the power and influence of the church on our world.

The third problem with camping at the prison is that we inevitably never follow the guide to our destination. We simply camp and wait for the rapture, never coming to the place of having Christ formed in us! Many think Paul's main focus was evangelism, but Paul was concerned with growing the church to reach her full potential. "My little children, for whom I labor in birth again until Christ is formed in you" (Galatians 4:19). "Him we preach, warning every man and teaching every man in all wisdom, that we may present every man perfect in Christ Jesus. To this end I labor." (Colossians 1:28–29)

Paul was concerned about Christians reaching their full potential. The law is concerned with requiring people to obey a standard. Grace is concerned with empowering people to reach their destiny. A prison guard keeps people bound for a certain time. Now that the time has come (Jesus has come), we are to follow the guide, whose focus is on leading people safely to the destination.

The Kingdom and the Guide

The guide is the Holy Spirit, but the answer to our dilemma is the kingdom of God. So, what is the connection? The kingdom is located in the Holy Spirit: "…for the kingdom of God is not a matter of eating and drinking, but righteousness and peace and joy in the Holy Spirit" (Romans 14:17). The word *kingdom* can best be described as the King's domain. Wherever the King has dominion, you will find the Holy Spirit administrating that dominion. When the kingdom comes, the Spirit has come; where the Spirit is Lord, the kingdom is expressed. Although they are different in their theological definitions, they are always together. Therefore, if we neglect, ignore, or reject the guide, we then neglect, ignore, and reject the kingdom of God.

"From that time Jesus began to preach and to say, 'Repent, for the kingdom of heaven is at hand'" (Matthew 4:17). There is a connection between repenting and the kingdom. Jesus told Nicodemus, "Unless one is born again, he cannot see the kingdom of God" (John 3:3). We know that in order to be born again one must first repent. So, we can conclude from these verses that one must repent to get into the kingdom. Peter later builds on our understanding, "Repent therefore and be converted, that your sins may be blotted out, so that times of refreshing may come from the presence of the Lord" (Acts 3:19). We see here that repenting gets us into the presence, again reinforcing the close connection between the kingdom of God and the Holy Spirit.

You Can Only Choose One

One way to tell which method of relating to God you are embracing is how you deal with others. A.W. Tozer once said, "The most important thing about a person is what they believe to be true about God."

If a person embraces the guard, he will more than likely be a guard to others—constantly watching people's behaviors to judge and condemn them based on their actions. If a person embraces the guide, he will guide others to God. A person under the guide will come alongside someone and help them reach their full potential. Some people believe their role is to protect God from being corrupted by sinners. Our true role is to guide others to God; God can guard Himself!

We must choose: guard or guide. Only one is valid in New Testament Christianity, only one is life giving. The guard will leave you dead, but probably comfortable. Dead people usually do not cause problems. They simply stay in graves and, as long as everyone "acts right," the dead will not cause any problems. Or you can choose the guide. Following the guide will bring risk, adventure, and uncomfortable situations. It is always uncomfortable when stepping into the unknown.

But do not be afraid; the guide has been called the Comforter, because when a person follows the guide, he is going to be uncomfortable at some point. Climbing with the guide is rewarding and the only way to arrive at your destiny. The journey with the guide will be a wild one, but you are sure to experience the life of Christ the whole time. You can be sure that quitters and campers will mock you and call you names. Do not worry. You simply remind them that there is more to the journey that they are not seeing. God will call you good and faithful.

A SLOW DEATH

After we realize what the problem is, we must determine how we arrived here so we do not repeat the mistake. I would like to address four factors that I believe contribute to the present crisis: we have misunderstood the nature of truth, misunderstood Jesus's coming; therefore, misunderstood the commission, and overreacted to error.

Understanding Truth

And you shall know the truth and the truth shall make you free.

John 8:32

Truth brings life. Jesus said that His words, which are truth, were spirit and life. Truth is absolutely central to relating to God, but many do not understand much about the nature of truth. There are two aspects that I wish to cover now and will discuss further later. First, all truth is layered. Second, truth is meant to be experienced.

All Truth Is Not Created Equal

Truth is not relative, but it is layered—layered like an onion. A person can peel back a layer of onion and be closer to the center, but what they are looking at is still an onion. In the same way, a person can be lead to a deeper truth. For example, "sin deserves death" is true, but deeper still is the truth of redemption, that sinners do not have to die because Jesus died for them. God shared a truth with us in the Old Testament and then a deeper one in the New Testament. In the Old Testament, if you touched a leper you became unclean. Why? The message is how easy it is to be contaminated (changed) by sin. But in the New Testament, Jesus touches the leper, and the leper changes—he becomes clean. Why? Because the greater truth is how powerful righteousness is over sinfulness. Likewise, if you touched a dead person, then you became unclean, but when Jesus touched a dead person, they were raised to life. God is building on previous truths!

Another example is when Jesus said to the disciples, "No longer do I call you servants…but I have called you friends" (John 15:15). Was Jesus saying they were to no longer serve? By no means. However, He was building on one truth by adding a deeper truth. Many in the church oppose what God is doing, because they think it opposes what they believe—or have been taught they should believe—as truth. However, it could be that God is adding to the truth they have embraced by building on it.

The gospel of the kingdom seems to oppose the gospel of salvation that many grew up hearing. It appears this way because of our misunderstanding of the nature of truth. The good news that people can be cleansed of their sin and restored to right relationship with God is just the start. The good news of the kingdom does not undo that or in any way take away from that reality; it is going deeper into the truth of our redemption. It does not have to oppose the truth of salvation, but it is God—in His timing—peeling back the layers.

I would like point out that nowhere in the New Testament will one find the phrase "gospel of salvation;" however, Jesus refers to the "gospel of the kingdom" at least twice (Matthew 25:14, Mark 1:14). I am not saying that there is no good news of being ransomed from sin and hell. God forbid! What I am saying is that salvation is only the beginning of the message of the good news of the kingdom. The good news of salvation is the door out of the prison and into the kingdom; the rest is the journey with the guide! Many have not made the transition from law to grace, because they think the revelation of grace is inconsistent with their understanding of the law. God is not inconsistent with Himself; He is simply building on a previous truth.

God is a very smart person. God has given us plenty of truth in the Scriptures, but in His mercy, He does not give us the entire revelation at one time. He knows we cannot handle it. "I still have many things to say to you, but you cannot bear them now" (John 16:12). Jesus withheld telling the disciples the whole truth, because He knew that they could not handle it. With truth comes responsibility. God will reveal to us truth as He sees we can handle it. He remembers we are but dust! However, many oppose His truth, not because they are rebellious or stubborn (well, not all), but because they have never been taught that truth is layered. God has shown us the beautiful truth of salvation by grace, through faith, and now is revealing to us the wonderful truth of the kingdom.

Isaac Newton discovered gravity; he did not create it. The concept of gravity existed from the beginning and was revealed to Newton. In the same manner, we are not discovering "new" truths, but ones that have been there all along; we are simply able to bear the revelation and responsibility better now. Every believer knows how this works: you have read a verse of Scripture your entire life, but one day it simply "clicks," and it means something different to you today. The revelation was always there but God, in His timing, showed you at the appropriate time.

Jesus continued in John 16 by saying, "However, when He, the Spirit of truth, has come, He will guide you into all truth" (John

16:13). Notice that He does not say when the Scriptures come, or when the New Testament is finished, or when the cannon is closed you will understand. No, He says when the Spirit of truth comes, He will guide us into all truth. Truth is always revealed by the Holy Spirit—never stumbled upon but guided to.

Why is this important? Glad you asked. It has been pointed out, "Faith comes by hearing, not by having heard." Faith is based on hearing God in the present tense. Let me give you an example that will show you the danger of misunderstanding layers of truth. God told Abraham to sacrifice Isaac, but later God said the opposite, "Do not lay your hand on the lad" (Genesis 22:12). I bet Isaac is glad Abraham kept listening to God!

If Abraham would have kept doing what God had said at the expense of what God was currently saying to him, he would have been guilty of the blood of Isaac. In the same way, when the church clings to what God has said at the expense of what He is currently saying, the church sacrifices its future on the altar of its traditions. The church then becomes guilty of murdering its young and its future. The church then dies and looks to God and wonders why He would allow such a thing. Or we create a theology that makes our defeat and ineffectiveness "God's will for the end times," which in turn eases our conscience and removes any responsibility away from us and makes fruitlessness somehow pleasing to God.

God was saying something in the Old Testament and built on that in the New Testament, which made the message different— complete. The Old Testament message was incomplete; it needed Jesus. For example, the Old Testament pointed out how horrible sin is; the New Testament pointed out how powerful grace and love are. It is incorrect exegesis to look at an Old Testament principle without seeing it through the lens of Christ. For example, David sinned with Bathsheba, and God struck his child with sickness, and the child died. The principle is simple: the wages of sin is death. Yet to look at this story and conclude that today God gives sickness and kills babies is an incorrect interpretation. The correct one would be seeing this analogy in light of redemption: "My sin deserved death, but Jesus died for me and as me; therefore, God does not kill babies, because it is unjust to pay for a sin twice. If we cling to the guard rather than embracing the guide, we will be guilty of killing our future!

"But the word of the Lord was to them, 'Precept upon precept, line upon line'" (Isaiah 28:13). God's Word (truth) comes line upon line, precept upon precept. That means it is building in layers. Through Martin Luther, God revealed justification by faith; with John Wesley, the Spirit revealed mass evangelism and the importance of holiness; and at Azusa Street, He revealed the beauty of the gifts. Line upon line. With John Wimber, He unveiled that all the saints "get to do the stuff,"(walk in the miraculous) and now the Spirit is unveiling the reality of His kingdom!

The Invitation to Revelation

Secondly, truth is meant to be experienced. The verse at the start of the section (John 8:32) uses the word *know*. This word in the Greek means "to experientially know, like a husband knows his wife." The truth that you experientially know will set you free. Jesus shows us this principle in His statements concerning the Pharisees, "You search the Scriptures, for in them you think you have eternal life; and these are they which testify of Me. But you are not willing (refuse) to come to Me that you may have life" (John 5:39–40). This is a monumental revelation! Jesus points out that when you study the Scriptures, you receive revelation. This revelation is an invitation to come to Jesus and experience the person of truth. Every revelation is an invitation to experience Jesus.

Some pastors and churches have good theory and theology, but never experience the person of truth through the Spirit of truth, which is partly the reason for the present death among churches. People are leaving our churches because there have not been actual encounters with truth, only sermons about it. This present generation and those to come will be generations that ask to see the fruit. God is ready to give us encounters. We must say yes to the invitation of God to experience truth. If you read through the book of Romans, you will come to the revelation that the just shall live by faith—that is an open-ended invitation to experience being justified by faith.

All truth is layered. God in His mercy withholds the deeper truth until we can bear it. We must not oppose something that seems to contradict the truth we know, but humbly seek God and ask if what we seek is simply a truth that He is building upon. Remember, if we cling to what God did say at the expense of what He is saying, we kill our young on the altar of our traditions. Truth is meant be experienced. Every revelation is an invitation to encounter Jesus. The truth of the kingdom of God has not been embraced largely because it appeared to oppose our beliefs; it does not oppose but rather builds on what we believe.

The First Coming of Christ

The Jewish people understood that when the Messiah came, He would come as a king with His kingdom. This is why the crowd received Jesus with palm branches. Before the Star of David a palm branch was Israel's national symbol. In 1 Kings 6, we read that Solomon decorated the temple with palm branches, and in Isaiah 9, a palm branch is cut down to symbolize the judgment of Israel.

When the crowd threw them in front of Jesus, it was not a simple sign of victory, but a realization that He was the Messiah and that He was going to restore the kingdom to Israel. That is why in Acts 1, the disciples misunderstand Jesus when He was talking about the kingdom. Jesus taught on the kingdom and then on the Holy Spirit, and the disciples just had to ask, "Lord, will You at this time restore the kingdom to Israel?" (Acts 1:6).

Furthermore, the issue of the kingdom is the only problem the

Romans had with Jesus. The Romans had a polytheistic view of the divine—they had thousands of gods. They were not upset that Jesus was claiming to be a god; however, they were clear that there was only one king and it was Caesar! When Jesus stood before Pilate, he was asked, "Are You the King of the Jews?" (John 18:33). To this, Jesus answered, "My kingdom is not of this world. If My kingdom were of this world, My servants would fight, so that I should not be delivered to the Jews; but now My kingdom is not from here" (John 18:36).

Jesus meant that His kingdom is not an earthly kingdom (from here), but a spiritual kingdom that embraces people from all races, nations, tribes, and tongues. Jesus continues with a very profound statement, "You say rightly that I am a king. For this cause I was born, and for this cause I have come into the world, that I should bear witness to the truth. Everyone who is of the truth hears My voice" (John 18:37).

Many have an incomplete understanding of the first coming of Christ. Redeeming mankind is one of the reasons Jesus came, but not the only reason. To really understand, we have to go back and understand what was given up in the garden. Not only did sin enter the world, but Adam forfeited his dominion that God had given him. The Bible teaches in Romans 6:16 that we are a slave to whomever we obey. God gave dominion of earth to Adam, and when he sinned, Adam handed that dominion over to the devil.

In Matthew 4:1–11, we find Jesus being tempted by the devil. In verses 8–9 we read, "Again, the devil took Him up on an exceedingly high mountain, and showed Him all the kingdoms of the world and their glory. And he said to Him, 'All these things I will give You if You will fall down and worship me.'" Jesus does not argue with the devil and say, "They are not yours to give." He simply rebukes him. The devil even knew why Jesus had come and was trying to persuade Him into recapturing the kingdoms without going to the cross. The Bible says that Jesus was tempted. You cannot be tempted by something that you do not believe is possible. I will never be tempted to pick a car up and carry it home. Why? Because

I can't! In order for Jesus to be tempted, Jesus had to believe the devil possessed the kingdoms of the earth to give to Him.

Jesus came to seek and save that which was lost—not just the people, but also the dominion that Adam lost. This idea of God losing dominion bothers people, because some believe that it violates God's sovereignty. It does not violate His sovereignty but, in fact, proves it. He knew from the beginning that the dominion would be lost, and He knew He would recapture it. Many think that if God is not in control then He is not God. That is not true. God can allow me to make all my own decisions and still work out His will in the end; that is true sovereignty. If He is not in control of every little thing, He will not cry and throw a tantrum. The devil having dominion of the earth does not mean that God could not pull the plug and crush the cosmos and start again. He could have done that, but He did not. He chose to come down as man and get it back!

Furthermore, Paul calls the devil the "god of this age" in 2 Corinthians 4:4, and Jesus calls him the "ruler of this world" in John 14. When Jesus rose from the dead and commissioned the disciples He said, "All authority has been given to Me in heaven and on earth," (Matthew 28:18)—which implies He won the dominion back! 1 John 3:8 lets the cat out of bag by claiming, "For this purpose the Son of God was manifested, that He might destroy the works of the devil." Everything that Jesus did—from preaching, to teaching, to healing the sick, to dying on the cross and rising again—was to destroy the devil's work and, in doing so, redeem mankind.

The reason that Jesus came was to bring with Him the kingdom of God. The king showed up with His kingdom. He did not come to save man so that "one day" they will see the kingdom, but to redeem mankind and bring them into the kingdom—right now! This is what marked His message: "Repent, for the kingdom is at hand" or has now become available (Matthew 4:17). He brought to us the good news that the wonderful kingdom of God is touchable, reachable, and now!

Understanding the Great Commission

"Go therefore and make disciples of all nations, baptizing them in the name of the Father and of the Son and of the Holy Spirit, teaching them to observe all things that I have commanded you" (Matthew 28:19–20). When we conclude that the only reason Jesus came was to save sinners, we might then conclude that the great commission is only to go save sinners, but in the Greek, the main verb of this sentence is not *go* but *teach*. Teach is connected to the word *obey*. The focus of the great commission is not for understanding, but for obedience: action. The verse is not saying, "Go and teach everyone how to understand salvation." We have reduced the great commission to "Go and teach them to understand, and lead as many people in a prayer as possible." But the gist of this verse is to obey. Obeying has to do with action. What is it we are to teach people to obey? "Everything that I have commanded you" (Matthew 28:20). The disciples were commissioned to make more disciples, and those next disciples were to do all that Jesus had commanded the original twelve to do.

I was pondering this one day and was overwhelmed by a passage repeated in almost every gospel. "These twelve Jesus sent out and commanded them, saying:…'as you go, preach, saying, "The kingdom of heaven is at hand." Heal the sick, cleanse the lepers, raise the dead, cast out demons'" (Matthew 10:5–8). Jesus commissioned the disciples to teach every disciple to do all that He had commanded them, which included heal the sick, cleanse the lepers, raise the dead, cast out demons, and preach the gospel of the kingdom. The point of the commission is not to make converts but disciples; disciples who preach the message of the kingdom and walk in the supernatural. This does not mean that the practical is not also done—giving a cup of cold water, clothing the naked, and feeding the poor. A true disciple should be doing the practical radically and the supernatural naturally.

Believers vs. Disciples

Many do not know that there is a difference between a believer and a disciple. The focus has been on getting people saved, which means our focus has been on making believers—but our commission is to make disciples. "Then Jesus said to those Jews who believed Him, 'If you abide in My word, you are My disciples indeed. And you shall know the truth, and the truth shall make you free'" (John 8:31–32). There were people who believed but were not disciples. To be a disciple is to abide (dwell, live) in truth. To do that one must be in close connection with the Holy Spirit, the one who guides us into all truth. A person cannot abide without the guide! Truth is not learned simply by intellectual gymnastics, but through the unveiling (revelation) of the Holy Spirit.

Disciples are people who can stand the scalpel of truth—truth that cuts straight to the problem and addresses it. Truth divides bone and marrow, even dives into the intentions of the heart. A person who can remain (abide) still while the Spirit uses truth to cut apart and address the intentions of the heart will move from a believer to a disciple.

True revelation opens the eyes of our heart and produces profound change. Cognitive understanding is information in the head that contributes to our intellect but does not produce change. This is how Paul can speak of some men as "always learning and never able to come to the knowledge of the truth" (2 Timothy 3:7). Those men learned intellectually but did not have knowledge of truth, because truth is only revealed by the Holy Spirit.

Reacting to Errors

"Everyone makes mistakes." A common statement, usually made by the person who just made the mistake. However, when people in the church make mistakes, we often imprison everything that person has taught behind a locked door of "Heresy." I would like to suggest that God always gives truth with the knowledge that people may reject it. He does this because He values the freedom of giving people choices.

Many people react when a truth is misapplied or distorted and "throw the baby out with bath water." I have had many of these experiences. One was with the Word of Faith movement. For years I had a deep dislike for the Word of Faith movement and its leader, Kenneth Hagin. I have since repented for hatred of a human being, much less a brother in Christ. What I discovered, as I studied, was that I disagreed with a pastoral application of a simple truth: God's Word is true regardless of what my senses tell me. I do not agree with all that Hagin taught; however, I do agree that God's Word is the ultimate reality regardless if I see it, taste it, touch it, or feel it. I can receive all of His promises by faith, apart from experience, and then allow Him to manifest (perform) His promises in His time.

No denomination is without fault. I have seen many misapplications of truth in my denomination, but I overlooked them while holding tight to my dislike for another group. What I had done was take one pastor's application of a truth and place (or misplace) his interpretation on a whole group and then call the truth itself heresy. Doing that was easier than admitting I did not care enough to try to understand. Plus, I did not have to worry about being labeled by my peers. Many believe Martin Luther was anti-Semitic, but does that mean his teaching on justification by faith alone was inaccurate? No! Why? Because the basis for his revelation was taught in the Scriptures.

Counterfeiting Pennies

The point has been made, and I would like to reinforce it: reaction (or overreaction) to an error only breeds more error! If you suspect the devil is counterfeiting moves of the Spirit, then I would like to submit a question: Does anyone counterfeit mere pennies? No! A thief counterfeits the valuable. The devil is working hard to counterfeit healing, prophecy, and other gifts of the Holy Spirit because they are valuable. I have come to the conclusion that cessationalists (those who believes the gifts—or *certain* gifts—have ceased with the death of the last apostle) are arrogant enough to believe that the great commission can be accomplished without the Holy Spirit giving us all of the gifts He gave to the body of Christ. Many fail to follow the Holy Spirit because of an overreaction to other people's beliefs instead of an intentional and in-depth study of Scripture.

Many in the broader church community have neglected, resisted, and quenched the Holy Spirit and His moving because many have failed to see that truth has layers. And God is still building! God is building on our understanding of Jesus's first coming and the great commission. We must not let the errors of others keep us from humbly and passionately pursuing the Holy Spirit and the kingdom!

The Coming Renewal and Reformation

Reformation is different than renewal or revival. Renewal has to do with going back and making something new, like restoring an old car. Revival is synonymous with an awakening. But reformation is about re-forming. Not simply refreshing or putting on a fresh coat of paint, but remodeling; the form and model takes on a new shape. The church needs to experience renewal and revival, being brought back to life, then needs reformation because the present form has contributed to our death. I want to share what I believe to be some of the changes that are to take place.

I believe the present death in our churches is causing people to ask, "Is this really all there is?" In searching for the answer to that question, many will embrace the message and enactment of the kingdom of God. The beginning of this movement of God will start with a deep repentance for how we have treated and interacted with the person of the Holy Spirit. This will be a time of humbleness and brokenness that will lead to an embracing of the gifts and the kingdom.

The embracing of the gifts will bring about a revolution. This revolution will consist of the everyday saint walking in the supernatural. There will not be some famous man who leads this great movement. This movement of God will be in relation to His entire body. Everyone in His kingdom is a prince or princess, priest or priestess. Every saint, old and young, will begin to walk in the purity and power of God, in partnership with the Holy Spirit.

This day of the saints will cause some magnificent transitions in the church. For many decades, the focus of the church has been on its services. We have become trained in putting on the best event of the week. However, with this moving of God among His people, that will begin to change. The people will begin to take the supernatural and the radically practical love of God into their homes and jobs. Then God-encounters or kingdom-sightings will take place in restaurants and marketplaces, wherever the saints go. In doing so, the kingdom of God will impact businesses, education, media, government, entertainment—resulting in one of the greatest reformations of all time, and we have the privilege of being a part of it!

The focus of churches will shift from services to relationships: relationship with God the Holy Spirit, and experiencing God in our relationships with others. In the expansion of the early church, radically transformed blacksmiths, fisherman, and carpenters spread the kingdom of God. This time it will be politicians, bankers, CEOs, farmers, secretaries, teachers, and housewives walking in the practical and supernatural, spreading the love of the King and His kingdom.

The question then arises: how do we get there?

THE WAY TO RESURRECTION

THE NEED FOR RENEWAL

The Downward Spiral of Rebellion

Reformation always starts with an individual and ends up impacting nations. However, the need for reformation stems from rebellion. Even the initial need for redemption was because of Adam and Eve's rebellion. Where there has been no rebellion, there is no need for renewal or reformation. This is a hard truth, but it is the start of the beginning of returning to God.

We will be examining how God brought reformation to the Israelites in Judges chapter 6. There seems to be a particular pattern throughout the book of Judges—a pattern of rebellion. It starts with the people of God walking in purity and power with the manifested presence of God (revival). From this place, the people of God move into apathy. Apathy creeps in when the people of God exchange the presence of God for traditions, idols, and formulas. From apathy, they transition into compromise, where the people of God become deceived and lower the standards of the Scriptures and righteous living.

No one ends up deceived who did not first compromise. Bill

Johnson once said, "Compromise is the welcome mat for deception." Next, the people of God spiral into a lifestyle of sin. This is when the people of God openly embrace evil, calling it good. From there, they goes downward into bondage where a repeated pattern of sin invites the devil and his kingdom to stay. In this state, freedom is sacrificed. The people of God lose the ability to choose. In Judges 6:1–6, the Israelites lost their ability to choose.

Defeat comes next. This happens when one loses the ability to overcome, to come out on top. Israel cannot beat or even defend themselves against the Midianites and the Amalekites. Furthermore, rebellion leads to emptiness, which is the loss of fulfillment. The Israelites were sowing and hardly reaping anything in return. Nothing they did seemed to satisfy! And last comes despair. Despair occurs when people lose hope. Hopelessness is always a sign that the kingdom of darkness has a strong hold. Any area of your life that does not have hope is an area where you are believing the lies of the enemy.

The Root of the Problem

It took the Israelites about seven years to come to the conclusion that the real problem did not lie anywhere except in their rebellion and relationship with God. They probably originally thought they had a political problem, or a financial problem, or a military problem, but all the while it was a God problem (or a lack-of-God problem)! The Israelites became good at coping. At first they coped with the subtle absence of intimacy with God, then a certain loss of focus and fulfillment, and finally a domineering, occupying army in their homeland, hunger, treachery and more. But now they had come to the point where they couldn't continue to cope. They were "brought very low because of Midian, and the sons of Israel cried to the Lord" (Judges 6:6, NASB). Amazingly, it was at the precise moment that Israel gave up on coping with their problems that they entered the process of renewal that would eventually release them from their overwhelming dilemma.

Today, like Israel of old, people are often quite adept at coping. They cope with loneliness, addictions, bad marriages, rebellious children, work stress, etc. Reformation starts when you quit coping and start calling out. Why did it take seven years before Israel called out to God? Before you judge them too harshly, consider why it is taking you so long to act on your need for God to deliver you from those things you were never meant to cope with.

Some Christians think their marriage is on the rocks because they have a communication problem, or a parenting disagreement, or a financial issue. That could be possible, but their primary problem may be a God problem. Some churches think they have an outreach problem, worship problem, "inreach" problem, tithing problem, attendance problem, a pastor problem, or a deacon problem—but really, it is a God problem. Some think our national crisis is a political problem, job shortage problem, economical problem … but it is a God problem. It is a problem between us and God. It is a rebellion problem that stretches back to the Garden of Eden. It is time that we stop merely coping and start calling out. It is time we quit reaching for all the resources that promise better results, and start crying out to God.

Israel's difficulty was their own rebellion and, after seven years of coping, they had finally had enough and began to cry out to God! What about you? Any area of your life that is not experiencing the life of Christ is an area where renewal is needed.

THE BIRTHPLACE OF REFORMATION

The Israelites did evil in the sight of the Lord. In Judges 6:6 we read, "So Israel was greatly impoverished because of the Midianites, and the children of Israel cried out to the Lord." One of the important starting places of revival is crying out to God—the realization that our present reality is not God's best for us. The reality that abundant life is available makes the taste of any circumstance less than that standard frankly unbearable.

This is how renewal started for me. I began to study the kingdom of God, looking up every scripture and trying to understand its meaning. I began to notice that Jesus referred to the kingdom over a hundred times in four gospels, but only mentions the church three times (Matthew 16, 18), and being born-again once (John 3). His first sermon was, "Repent, for the kingdom of heaven is at hand." (Matthew 4:17) His last moments with the disciples were spent teaching them about "things pertaining to the kingdom of God. (Acts 1:3) I realized that the kingdom of God was the focus of Jesus and the whole point of the New Testament. Salvation was the door, the entryway, into the kingdom.

All of this was a grand and rich discovery. However, I ran into one verse that stopped me cold in my tracks and pulled apart the ignorant "paradise" (really a desert, I just did not know it) I had been living in. The verse was one I had memorized and quoted, but in light of my study on the kingdom, it introduced a whole new dynamic. "For the kingdom of God is not in word but in power!" (1 Corinthians 4:20). With my mouth open in amazement, jaw resting clear down on my desk, I realized I had been trained and educated and was quite comfortable with the Word but knew nothing about the power. I only knew how to talk!

Next, my mind raced to 1 Corinthians 2:4–5 where Paul says,

> And my speech and my preaching were not with persuasive words of human wisdom, but in demonstration of the Spirit and of power, that your faith should not be in the wisdom of men but in the power of God.

I trembled as I reflected on my ministry and how all I had to offer people were "wise and persuasive" words!

Notice in 1 Corinthians 2:4, Paul never said he did not preach. He did say that his preaching resulted in a "demonstration of the Spirit and of power." Often when I finished preaching, many would compliment me (probably just being nice), but there was little demonstration in their feedback of God's power, if any. So, hear me, I am not saying that there is no need for biblical, Spirit-filled preaching and teaching—that would be an unscriptural and heretical overreaction. What I am saying is that preaching and teaching was all I had to offer! I had stopped short of what God had for me. Knowing that there was a reality of power available to me and that God wanted me to walk in it was enough to bring me to my knees to cry out for this expression of the kingdom in my life. I cried out for this power night and day, till it became the unconscious ring of my heart. The point is that the realization that there was more made my present reality unbearable. That is what happens when you taste of God.

God answers the Israelites by sending a prophet. However, the prophet did not prophesy about the future but reminded them of their history with God. The sermon that the prophet brought was only about twenty seconds long, and yet it was exactly what they needed. It was precise and it was powerful. It cut through all the theories and excuses as well as all the defeat and delay. It contained the key to understanding the times and became the turning point that brought a nation face-to-face with the heart of man's problem in every age. It is worth the effort to understand its message.

First, this prophet's sermon reminded the Israelites of the goodness of God by reviewing three basic things:

(1) how God brought them out of Egypt,

(2) how God blessed them with the Promise Land, and

(3) how God made a covenant with them.

In verse 8 of Judges 6, the prophet reminds the people of how God redeemed (brought out) Israel from the Egyptians. In verse 9, the prophet reminds them that God "gave you their land (blessed)." Then in verse 10, the prophet recalls, "I am the Lord your God." This statement is a reminder of the covenant.

Ninety percent of this simple sermon on renewal was about God—how good He is and what He had done for Israel. All experiences of renewal will be an awakening to the goodness of God. Remembering what God has done for us and how good He has been to us positions us to understand His rebuke.

Then came the remaining ten percent of the sermon. The prophet pointed to the place of the Israelites' departure from God. "Also I said to you, 'I am the Lord your God; do not fear the gods of the Amorites, in whose land you dwell.' But you have not obeyed My voice" (Judges 6:10). The sin of Israel was idolatry (the worshiping of other gods).

However, in our modern culture, idols do not come in golden or wooden statues. For our day, idolatry results when we value the temporal more than the eternal. What you value is where your heart is (Luke 12:34). Materialism is the turning of the heart toward temporal things rather than eternal things. For example, if we had someone who was running for public office who had an immoral stance but who promised prosperity, many in the church would vote for him. Supporting this candidate is putting money (temporal) above morals (eternal)—idolatry. Idolatry always starts with materialism—the affections of the heart turned towards the temporal instead of the eternal.

Israel's sin was idolatry, but the commandment they broke was that of fearing other gods. I hope the principle does not escape your notice: you will worship what you fear. Fear affects and redirects our worship. People who fear going broke worship money. People who fear people's opinions worship their reputation. People who fear failure worship success.

To me, worship is seen in where you "ship" your "worth." What you determine as being of worth is what you have worshipped. When we fear, we apply worth to the object feared. When we fear, we tether ourselves to the object and make decisions with the feared thing in mind. Thus we are worth-shiping it. For this reason one of the most repeated commands in the Bible is, "Fear not." Another is to "Fear the Lord your God."

The point of the prophet's message is to show the Israelites where to begin. Repentance is the foundation. We must make our repentance firm so that our foundation will be solid. John the Baptist preached about the need to bear fruit of repentance (Luke 3:8). This is a way of making our repentance sure. If I have bitterness toward someone and the Lord brings conviction, I acknowledge my sin and pray for forgiveness. Then I go to the person and ask them to forgive me. This is bearing fruit of my repentance. When our Lord Jesus visited Zacchaeus' house, Luke records Zacchaeus saying, "Look, Lord, I give half of my goods to the poor; and if I have taken anything from anyone by false accusation, I restore fourfold." (Luke 19:8) Jesus responded, "Today salvation has come to this house ..." (Luke 19:9) Jesus can make this statement because of the fruit of repentance that Zacchaeus has shown. Bearing fruit of repentance is important. It gives a firm foundation for the Lord to build on, while also protecting us from the enemy's attack. When the enemy (Satan) comes to try to accuse us, we will have fruit to remind him that we have repented.

In order to experience renewal, we must stop trying to cope or handle our problems and start crying out to the Lord. We must become broken before God. We must listen as He shows us our place of departure. When we hear it, we must humble ourselves and repent. The church that God is raising up in this hour will be one who fears no man, loves not their own lives unto death, and fears God only!

Renewal Starts with One

In Judges 6:11–24, Israel realized a need for renewal and began to cry out to God. God replied through His prophet, pointing His people back to the place of departure. Let's look at how He brings renewal to a person. We find Gideon threshing wheat in a winepress in order to hide it from the Midianites. Then the angel of the Lord appears to Gideon and says, "The Lord is with you, you mighty man of valor!" (v. 12). God halts the normalcy with a call to greatness. However, Gideon responds in an interesting way—he begins to argue!

> If the Lord is with us, why then has all this happened to us? And where are all His miracles which our fathers told us about, saying, 'Did not the Lord bring us up from Egypt?' But now the Lord has forsaken us and delivered us into the hands of the Midianites.
>
> Judges 6:13

When the angel said, "The Lord is with you," Gideon tried to change the subject to "if the Lord is with us." But God would not change the subject, not even to answer Gideon's questions.

I often have a similar problem. I want to talk about an issue, but God has determined to talk about something entirely different. Even though He is always patient, He will not change the subject. The sooner I can pick up on this and begin to pray with God, the more effective my prayer life becomes.

God ignored Gideon's questions and continued. "Go in this might of yours, and you shall save Israel from the hand of the Midianites. Have I not sent you?" (v. 14). Gideon responded with all the logical reasons why he could not do what God had told him he could do. "Indeed my clan is the weakest in Manasseh, and I am the least in my father's house" (v. 15). But the Lord answers Gideon's reasoning with, "I will be with you" (v. 16).

God called Gideon to the impossible, and Gideon wanted to know how it would happen. God answered, "I will be with you." This has been God's answer to the same question for all of history. Moses asked that question in Exodus 3, and God responded the same. This one simple truth is what started a national reformation. All renewal flows from a revelation of God's presence with us.

Moses understood it, Joshua was commanded to remember it (Joshua 1:1–9), and David said in Psalms 16:8, "I have set the Lord always before me." Of course, David did not have the power to pick God up and place God in front of him. He was saying he focused on God being with him. As Jesus said, "The Son can do nothing of Himself, but what He sees the Father do; for whatever He does, the Son also does in like manner." (John 5:19) All of these great saints, as well as our Savior, walked with an awareness and dependence upon the presence of God.

Every person I have seen experience personal renewal was one who simply said "yes" to God's invitation to a deep, meaningful, relationship. Rich intimacy with God is the fruit of the cross— "God was in Christ reconciling the world to Himself" (2 Corinthians 5:19). Removing our sin and reconciling us back to Himself was God's whole purpose of the cross.

Next, Gideon properly responded with a sacrifice: worship (v. 19). People who encounter God normally are not worried about how much it cost them, but instead are overwhelmed by the fact they just encountered God. Gideon brings an ephah amount of flour. In a time when Israel was impoverished, Gideon gave a great sacrifice. Worship always costs us something!

In verse 24, we find the end of the beginning: "So Gideon built an altar there to the Lord, and called it The-Lord-is-Peace." Renewal had come! God begins a national reformation by calling one man to complete dependence on Him. The altar is the beginning place of renewal. Our altar is not a pile of rocks or the front of a church building, but our personal relationship with God. As taught in Romans 12, the only reasonable response to God and His mercy is to put our bodies on the altar. Repenting for valuing and depending on other things, and learning to value the Spirit of God—entering into deep, rich, meaningful intimacy with God—is where all renewal starts. Renewal can only flow from His presence! It is all about Him, and life flows from Him.

We must say yes to this invitation. We must make the correct adjustments to our lives to value that presence and walk continually with our God. This means making time to simply be with Him, consulting Him before decisions, and waiting to hear from Him. There will be many things you will have to sacrifice to walk with Him, but I promise that when you arrive where He is taking you, it will all be worth it. I have never sacrificed anything to God that He has not given me something more valuable in return!

CONFRONTATION

Healthy confrontation is needed. Without it we would never change. Most of the time, the greatest change in our lives is the product of great confrontation. I can remember my first year of marriage. I remember thinking about my wife, "She is never going home … this is her home!" Our first year, like many marriages, was filled with struggles and hardships. However, it taught me some of the most valuable lessons and produced in me some of the most wonderful changes! Who I am today is partly related to how I responded to those confrontations.

In all renewal and reformation, God must confront us. He must confront the lies we believe with the power of His truth. Abundant life only comes from truth. Jesus said that His words (truth) were spirit and life. So for renewal to come, God must confront the strongholds with the truth. Let's examine how God does this.

Strongholds, according to 2 Corinthians 10:3–5, are any thoughts, imaginations, or high things that exalt themselves against the knowledge of God. Any "knowledge" that argues, challenges, or contradicts the wisdom of God must be confronted. Not in anger, or any other form of the flesh, but in love, with gentleness to the person.

For we do not wrestle against flesh and blood, but against principalities, against powers, against the rulers of the darkness of this age, against spiritual hosts of wickedness in the heavenly places.

Ephesians 6:12

Our confrontation is with the lies of Satan.

First, God confronts Gideon's strongholds. He does not do this by labeling him stupid or ignorant or by demanding repentance. God does this by calling Gideon to the impossible. Destiny always confronts apathy! When God calls us to the impossible, He confronts our self-centeredness. The call to the impossible brings an awareness of our inadequacies, which makes us vulnerable. When vulnerable, we become dependent on Him, which positions us to accomplish the impossible. Paul put it this way: when we are weak we are strong.

The constant reality that God has called us to the impossible keeps us reliant on Him. Jesus told His disciples, "I send you out as lambs among wolves" (Luke 10:3). That had to be a comforting thought! Yet what He was doing was showing them that they were being sent on an impossible mission. Staying close to the Shepherd would be the only way they would stay off the wolf's dinner plate.

Gideon believed a lie, which led him to feel disqualified for God's use. The lie is revealed in Gideon's response to the Lord, "My clan is the weakest in Manasseh, and I am the least in my father's house" (Judges 6:15). Gideon believed that his family, his stature, his reputation, or his personal history determined his identity! Where we come from or what we look like does not qualify or disqualify us for God's use. Our identity is determined by our Creator; we are whatever He says we are! God confronts this lie with one truth, "I will be with you." Gideon asks, "Who am I?" God answers, "That is not important, I will be with you." In essence God is saying, "Gideon, you're the guy I have chosen to hang out with."

God's presence with us is what qualifies us to do the impossible. It is not our education, family background, personal history, physical appearance, or our holiness, gifting, or talents; it is Him with us. Anything else is a false strength that is destined to crumble in due time.

Many in the church today have reduced ministry down to what is humanly possible. Fundraisers, feeding the poor, or mowing someone's lawn are all good things to do, but a Hindu or Buddhist could do them. A.W. Tozer once said, "If the Holy Spirit was removed from our churches, many would not notice any difference." Only doing what is humanly possible is simply the result of human effort. The most powerful argument that Christianity has for being the true religion is not Jesus's having been alive or Jesus dying on the cross. Buddha lived and died. Mohammed lived and died. Notice, neither of them lived or died like Jesus; however, the separation between Christianity and all other religions in the world is the reality of the resurrection!

Resurrection power is still the dividing point. Jesus lives! This impossibility of the dead coming alive again at the name of Jesus is still the mark of true Christianity. Dead marriages coming alive again. Dead churches, spiritually dead people, or dead rebellious teenagers coming alive with abundant life is the mark of the king and His kingdom. The dead being resurrected is the simplest form of kingdom expression and is what renewal is in its totality.

Jesus made powerless Christianity inexcusable. We either admit we are not living in the power that is available to us and start crying out to God, or we create a theology that reduces the model that Jesus left for us to one we can mimic without Him. Scripture shares how serious Jesus was about the issue of power in Acts 1:4, 8:

> He commanded them not to depart from Jerusalem, but to wait for the Promise of the Father…But you shall receive power when the Holy Spirit has come upon you; and you shall be witnesses to Me in Jerusalem, and in all Judea and Samaria, and to the end of the earth.

Notice Jesus commanded them to wait for this power. This shows us Jesus's seriousness concerning power. He was not afraid the disciples would not go to the ends of the earth. If He did not think they would, He would not need to command them to wait. However, He was concerned that they would go without power. Resurrection power is still what separates those who live in the kingdom of God from the rest of the world.

This resurrection power is impossible in and of man. This is why many in the church have reduced ministry down to what is humanly possible apart from full reliance on God. If we can do it ourselves, then we do not have to rely on God. We then can appear successful while still being dead! This is trading the presence of God for mere traditions or formulas—apathy, the first stage of rebellion!

Reformation in the Home

After God dealt with Gideon's strongholds, Gideon worshipped (Judges 6:23). Worship is always the response when His presence or Word is received. Out of this worship time, God spoke. Let me suggest to you that this is a great example of how to hear from God. If you struggle with hearing God, it may be that you have not done the last thing He said. So, worship. In worship you become open and sensitive to Him. Seek Him, cry out to Him, lavish love on Him, and wait. Do not put stipulations on your worship—just enjoy Him. I promise He will respond to a worshiper!

God dealt with Gideon through Gideon allowing the sword of the Spirit (the Word of God) to pierce his heart. Once the sword worked its way into Gideon's heart, Gideon was ready and able to take the handle of the sword and put it to use for the glory of God. Only when we have allowed the Word to pierce our hearts do we have a right to use the sword on others.

God spoke to Gideon but it was not something Gideon was crazy about hearing. God called Gideon to tear down the strongholds in his family,

> Now it came to pass the same night that the Lord said to him,
> 'Take your father's young bull, the second bull of seven years old,

and tear down the altar of Baal that your father has, and cut down the wooden image that is beside of it.

Judges 6:25

Renewal begins with one person, but before it comes to the nations, it must come to families. I am sure Gideon thought hard about God's request; this act could cost him his family. But the Bible says, "So Gideon took ten men from among his servants and did as the Lord had said to him. But because he feared his father's household and the men of the city too much to do it by day, he did it by night."

I have come to the conclusion that God is the most logical person of all time (literally). There is always good reason behind His words. He wants us to deal with strongholds and idols in our families for a purpose. The family was God's foundation for man. However goes the family, so goes the nation! It has been said, "Behind every great man is a surprised mother-in-law." (Ha ha, just kidding.) Behind every great man is someone who believed in him. For Gideon, it was the angel of the Lord who believed in him more than he did in himself. Jesus believed in the disciples, which created world-changers out of uneducated fishermen. We all need a place of encouragement and support, a place that is filled with hope that will enable dreams to be born. For some of us it is our church, for others it is a teacher or mentor, but God's first plan is for it to be the family. Some of our families' only hope of freedom and redemption is in us challenging the lies and the idols with the truth of God's Word. This is not to be done in a militant way but as Jesus did with the woman at the well (John 4)—with love, compassion, and with our ultimate goal of being connected to the love and life of God. Whether we do it overtly or covertly (Gideon went at night), we must confront and defeat the strongholds and idols that have been blinding and leaving our families hopeless.

The Twist of Obedience

In Judges 6:25, we see that the Israelites had turned to worshiping Baal. Baal was known as the god of prosperity. Israel valued being prosperous (temporal) more than keeping the covenant (eternal) they had made with Jehovah. Interestingly, we find that "Israel grew greatly impoverished because of the Midianites" (Judges 6:6). I hope this principle does not escape you: what they disobeyed God in order to obtain, they lost! To put it simply: anything you put above God you will eventually lose! I once knew a family who stopped coming to church to spend more time with their family. Now their family does not want anything to do with each other. This is not God being harsh; this is the downward spiral of sin. God holds all things together including our families—remove him, and it falls apart.

There is good news. Gideon obeyed God and tore down the stronghold in his family even though he risked losing all of them. And when the men of the city came for Gideon to punish him for his rebellion, "Joash (Gideon's father) said to all who stood against him, 'Would you plead for Baal? Would you save him? Let the one who would plead for him be put to death by morning! If he is as god, let him plead for himself…'" (Judges 6:31).

Gideon's father was defending Gideon. Not only do you lose the things you disobey God in order to obtain, but conversely, you inevitably obtain what you thought you were sacrificing in order to obey. I know of a husband who obeyed God in what could have been the sacrifice of his marriage, but God showed up, touched his wife, and gave him a renewed relationship and marriage!

Let me give you some practical tips on confronting strongholds in your family. First, and please listen, humility is where it starts! Repent to your family when God confronts your strongholds. Doing this gives them a grid with which they can start processing things. It softens you and them towards God's truth. Second, begin praying for your family, asking God to identify some family strongholds for you. They may not be far from your own. Third, be patient (but not passive). When you hear a lie spoken (anything contradicting God's Word), do not pass the opportunity to confront it with truth; however, be patient with your family as they change their thought processes. One may have to confront the same lie every day; that is okay. Confront it nonetheless! Fourth, remember God did not confront Gideon by yelling, screaming, calling him stupid, dumb, or through any other means of the flesh, but by encouraging Him into truth. Be a guide, not a guard, and remember that love never fails (1 Corinthians 13).

Next, we see that as Gideon confronted the stronghold in his family, he also was confronting the strongholds in a group or culture. "The men of the city said to Joash, 'Bring out your son that he may die, because he has torn down the altar of Baal, and because he has cut down the wooden image that was beside it,'" (Judges 6:30). I would like to suggest to you that most strongholds in your family will generally be strongholds that are also in your current culture. We see strongholds elsewhere in the Bible that affect entire groups, like in Ephesus where the practice of magic was widespread (Acts 19:19) or Jezebel's effects on the church (culture) in Revelation 2:20. The point that I believe the scripture is making is that there were three levels of strongholds confronted by God: strongholds in the mind, strongholds in the family, and strongholds in the people of God!

The lesson to be learned is two-fold and simple: be ready for healthy confrontation, and do not compromise your devotion to God for anything. It is foolishness to disobey God to try and maintain unity, or to protect a relationship, or because you do not understand. Surrender to the reality that whatever He says, regardless of what it appears to be, is the best thing for us! Last, notice the progression of renewal: crying out (enough is enough), God responds with a word, personal renewal in a person, and then renewal in the family. Let's look at what happens next.

THE ANOINTING

Then all the Midianites and Amalekites, the people of the East, gathered together; and they crossed over and encamped in the Valley of Jezreel. But the Spirit of the Lord came upon Gideon; then he blew the trumpet, and the Abiezrites gathered behind him.

Judges 6:33–34

The time had come for release, for the Israelites to be free from the bondage and unproductive life that their own rebellion had caused, and to enter into freedom and the higher quality of life that God intended for them to have. And where did the Lord start? The anointing! "But the Spirit came upon Gideon" (Judges 6:34). What a wonderful and powerful statement. Notice the comparison the Bible is making: all the armies of the Midianites and Amalekites moved closer to attack, but the Spirit fell on Gideon. It is like this verse is saying, "Oh, those poor Midianites and Amalekites, they do not know they're outnumbered!" You see, the Spirit of God resting on one person is a majority!

This statement does not mean that God was not with Gideon earlier in the story. This verse is describing a supernatural event called the anointing. My dear friend Jim Hylton has given one of the best descriptions of the New Testament anointing that I have heard, "The anointing is the Spirit of God coming upon an individual to draw out of that individual what He has put in them." The anointing comes upon us for a certain function that will always minister to others. It has been put this way, "God is in me for my sake, but comes upon me for others' sake."

In the Old Testament one can see the anointing coming upon Samuel, Saul, David, Joshua, Gideon, Samson, and others. The Bible is filled with the statement "the Spirit came upon." But in every case, the Spirit came upon a person for a certain purpose or function. In the New Testament we still see this principle at work; however, it is not as noticeable. But Jesus said, "The Spirit of the Lord is upon Me, because He has anointed Me to preach the gospel to the poor" (Luke 4:18). Notice the Spirit "coming upon" is the anointing, and it was for a certain purpose.

There is some confusion in the body of Christ in terms of the indwelling presence (Spirit) and the anointing of the Spirit. I believe the Scriptures teach that these two functions of the Spirit are different and separate acts. Let me give you an illustration. I am a believer. I have the Spirit of the resurrected Christ living in me, the same Holy Spirit as Billy Graham has living in him. However, I cannot go rent the biggest stadium in my town, draw an audience of thousands, and lead thousands to Christ tomorrow. (Not unless God commands me.) Why? Because although we have the same Spirit living inside of us, I do not have Dr. Graham's calling or anointing.

The Indwelling Spirit

It is at this point where the differences in pentecostals and traditional evangelicals become apparent. I do not wish to enter that debate here. What I do wish to show you is the teaching of the Scriptures pertaining to the anointing. Let's review that teaching with humility and wisdom.

In John 20, we discover a very interesting event, which, for many, goes unnoticed. It goes overlooked in our excitement of the resurrection and by our enthusiastic jump to the book of Acts. It is the Holy Spirit indwelling the disciples. In John 20:22, we read, "And when He had said this, He breathed on them, and said to them, 'Receive the Holy Spirit.'" The object received is the person of the Holy Spirit. But look at the language. "He breathed on them." This picture shows two important things. First, it is not said but implied that to receive this breath, one must breathe in! The picture is the Holy Spirit coming in. Second, it is a word picture of creation. The last time God breathed on someone it was for the purpose of bringing them to life (Genesis 2). This is a picture of the disciples receiving the Spirit, which is the administrator of eternal life.

It is at this point we can be certain that the disciples are saved. The qualification for being redeemed is two-fold: first, confess with your mouth that Jesus is Lord. The disciples had done that! Second, believe that God has raised Him from the dead. They had, only seconds earlier, stuck their hands in His side. So, we can check that off the list. They had met the qualifications for salvation (faith) according to Romans 10:9. However, the book of Romans also says,

> Now if anyone does not have the Spirit of Christ, he is not His … But if the Spirit of Him who raised Jesus from the dead dwells in you, He who raised Christ from the dead will also give life to your mortal bodies through His Spirit who dwells in you.
>
> Romans 8:9–11

I believe this is what took place in just one short verse. In breathing in the breath of Jesus, the disciples received the indwelling Holy Spirit, which administrated the work of Calvary, baptizing the disciples into His death, producing eternal life. Allow me to put it this way: if Peter would have died between John and Acts, he would have gone to heaven!

For the sake of argument, I would like to take a moment to address a confusing theory. Some have said that we do not know the time Jesus breathed on the disciples in relation to the Spirit falling in Acts 2. The logic goes like this: John and Acts were written by two different authors, and although John comes before Acts in our New Testament, it does not mean that they happened that way in real time. For example, the book of Matthew comes before Mark, but many scholars believe Mark was written first. So, this thought concludes that a person cannot argue the event in John happening before Pentecost because there is not an accurate timetable. However, I would like to make an observation that should help clarify this misconception.

One largely significant event has yet to happen in John's version, and we know it has happened by Luke's account of Acts 2. The event is the ascension of Christ. We know, according to Scriptures, that Christ's ascension took place before Acts 2 and we know that John 20 occurs chronologically before the ascension of Christ (because John records Jesus talking to the disciples). So from that one event we can conclude that John's account was pre-ascension and that Acts 2 was post-ascension. This gives us an accurate chronological table to work with—John's account came first, then later came Pentecost. This is important because it proves that the disciples had received the Holy Spirit before Pentecost.

Assuming this is true—the disciples received the Holy Spirit in John 20—then what was the purpose in Acts 2?

> It is not for you to know the times or seasons which the Father has put in His own authority. But you shall receive power when the Holy Spirit has come upon you; and you shall be my witnesses to Me in Jerusalem, and in all Judea and Samaria, and to the end of the earth.
>
> Acts 1:7–8

Do not let the small words escape your notice. In John 20, the disciples breathed the Spirit in, but here the Spirit "came upon"—two different functions, administered by the same Holy Spirit. In this verse, power is the object received, not the Holy Spirit. Also, notice the Spirit came upon those in the upper room for a specific function—in this case, witnessing.

The Bible records, "He (Jesus) commanded them not to depart from Jerusalem, but to wait for the Promise of the Father" (Acts 1:4). As stated earlier, Jesus was not afraid that the disciples would not go to the ends of the earth. He was afraid they would go without the anointing, without power! Again, trying not to be too redundant, let me repeat: in John 20, the person of the Holy Spirit is the object being received, and it was an internal event (notice there are no external manifestations of the Spirit in John 20). But in Acts 1:8, the object received is power, not the Holy Spirit. This power was received when the Holy Spirit came upon (not in) them.

Function and Anointing

The question that I want to submit is: Did Gideon receive the anointing because he obeyed God or because the enemy moved in close? I believe the answer is…yes. The Bible teaches that the Spirit is given to those who obey (Acts 5:32). And it also states, "When the enemy comes in like a flood, the Spirit of the Lord raises up a standard against him" (Isaiah 59:19). The only difference between this time and every other time the enemy had come to attack Israel is that the Spirit of God had someone to come upon. How did Gideon become that person?

The process moves like this: God's calling, Gideon's response, and God's provision. First, we find a sovereign act of God in calling Gideon to be used to defeat the Midianites. God did not choose to call Joe or Jim, but Gideon. There are many in the church today that are opposed to God's sovereign acts. The idea that God chooses certain people for certain tasks somehow offends some people's idea of a loving and fair God. In ignorance these people quote, "God is no respecter of persons." That verse is true, but He still calls some (not all) "to be apostles, some prophets, some evangelists, and some pastors and teachers." (Ephesians 4:11) Paul also put it this way, "Are all apostles? Are all prophets? Are all teachers? Are all workers of miracles?" (1 Corinthians 12:29). The answer is not stated but implied: no, not everyone has the same function.

Romans 12 is a chapter loved by many. For believers it is a call to a deeper life, one of surrender and transformation. I would like to point out a flow of thought Paul appears to be making in this famous chapter. In verse one, Paul starts with surrender. "Present your bodies a living sacrifice" (Romans 12:1). Next, he moves to the will with the command to "be not conformed." This is a choice of our will. We are to stop being conformed to the world and start being transformed by the renewing of the mind. Then Paul mentions being humble. "For I say, through the grace given to me, to everyone who is among you, not to think of himself more highly than he ought to think." Paul is pointing out that the first fruit of a renewed mind is humility.

Furthermore, Paul commands us to think soberly according to the measure of faith, and then states, "For as we have many members in one body, but all the members do not have the same function" (Romans 12:4). Paul then follows up with "Having then gifts…" Do not let these principles pass you by; Paul points out that every Christian has a function and has gifts to accomplish the function assigned.

I believe a person could conclude that Paul is teaching that the function is what must be determined. Gifting is important, but if I do not know what function my gift accomplishes, it will be useless, or at least not as productive as it was intended. When God calls us to something, we must respond by faith, and then we will have all we need to accomplish what He has assigned! "God is able to make all grace abound toward you, that you, always having all sufficiency in all things, may have an abundance for every good work" (2 Corinthians 9:8).

God is sovereignly calling every believer to a specific function in His body. There is not any appendix in the body of Christ. He has a place in the body for you. We must ask, seek, knock and worship. As we do, He will call us to certain functions; as we respond in faith, He will supply the anointing. I would like to insert a disclaimer. I have come to know God as both consistent yet spontaneous. He may give you a gift first and then tell you what the function is. The point I am making is that there is a standard in the Scripture—gifts are meant to minister to others.

Receiving the Anointing

Receiving is an interesting concept. There are many things in Scripture we are told to receive. Many do not know how to receive. In order to be a good receiver in football, one must have sensitive hands. Hard hands are not good for receiving. Hands that are responsive, yielding, and gentle will be hands that receive well. Imagine trying to receive an egg thrown at you. To effectively receive the egg one must have hands that are gentle—receiving the egg, with the egg in mind.

To receive the anointing, or to better receive the person of the Holy Spirit, one must be yielding and responsive to Him. Speaking of the Holy Spirit, it has been said, especially among classical evangelicals, "You cannot receive part of a person." I would like to suggest you cannot receive half a person but you can half-heartedly receive a person. Say a group of friends are playing cards around a table in one of their homes. Another friend walks through the front door. The group looks up at the person, acknowledging his presence by their glances but they go right back to playing without saying a word. The friend who walked in then walks to the table and sits down in a chair and waits for a new game to begin. Was the friend received? Well, he was not repelled or denied. But was he received well? No. Some treat the Holy Spirit this way. They tell Him, "Come in, sit down and be quiet, because I'm in a debate with a Pentecostal about how a person receives all of You, once, at salvation!" A person can hold and defend either theological stance and never really yield to the Holy Spirit. Surrender is the key to the anointing and to walking with the person Holy Spirit.

Under the Influence

Now that we have discussed the anointing, let us move on to being under the influence. What was the effects of the anointing on Gideon? We will discover what they are in Judges 6:34–35:

> But the Spirit of the Lord came upon Gideon; then he blew the trumpet, and the Abiezrites gathered behind him. And he sent messengers throughout all Manasseh, who also gathered behind him. He also sent messengers to Asher, Zebulun, and Naphtali; and they came up to meet them.

In this passage, we see two major effects of being under the influence of the anointing. First, boldness—Gideon blew the trumpet. This was a call to gather the people, a call to war. This was the guy who cowered down in the winepress. This is the guy who went to tear down his father's idols under the cover of night out of fear. But when the Holy Spirit fell upon him, the boldness rose within him.

Throughout the Bible one can find supernatural courage connected to the Holy Spirit. Often in the book of Acts, when the Holy Spirit filled someone for a certain function, it also brought great courage. Courage is important. All other virtues hinge on courage. A person can have the virtue of honesty but not have the courage to be honest. A person can have a deep spring of love but not possess the courage needed to become vulnerable in a relationship. The anointing can come upon us with courage and draw out of us those virtues that have been lying dormant.

Second, we find the anointing brought favor. The Abiezrites gathered behind Gideon, as did men from surrounding regions. I can see two reasons that point this out as being an act of supernatural favor. We know, according to Judges 7, that 32,000 men were prepared to follow Gideon into battle. To me this is a miracle. The men had faith in Gideon. Either they had never heard of him, which communicates to me favor—favor because these men are willing to be led into battle by a man they know nothing about! Or worse, they do know him! They know he is the smallest man from the weakest tribe, and still they followed! We see the anointing brought favor in Nehemiah's life, in Daniel's life, and even in Jesus's life. When God is for you, who can be against you? The only explanation for Israel's response is that, when the anointing comes, it brings supernatural favor. God truly makes all grace abound to us!

To tie all of these thoughts into a nice bundle, let me say that God has a sovereign call for you. Go before Him in worship, seeking, asking, knocking and waiting. He is more ready to speak than we are to hear. The anointing comes upon us to draw out of us what God has put in us to accomplish the function He has called us to. So, always seek for an anointing to match your calling. Remember, whatever God calls you to do—no matter how it appears—it is the best and safest place for you. And last, God is consistently reliable. He will make all grace abound to you that in all things, at all times, you will have more than enough to accomplish what He has assigned to you to accomplish! You do not have to worry about disappointing Him; you cannot disappoint a God who already knows everything! He knows the end from the beginning, He knows your weaknesses and your strengths, and He has made up His mind … He loves you!

THE PLACE OF GLORY

The person most passionate about the glory of the Lord is the Lord Himself. It would be wise for us to cultivate a passion for the glory, too. The Bible is filled with scriptures of God doing things for His name's sake, for His glory, that His people might know His goodness and glory. Even though "glory" is such a large word in the Scripture, many do not know much about it. The Hebrew and Greek words for glory cover a vast array of meanings, making it seemingly impossible to come to a solid conclusion of what "the glory" really is. In light of that, I would like to make a suggestion as to what God thinks His glory is.

In Exodus 32, God and Moses are chatting. God has been put out with His people and has come to the conclusion to kill them. But Moses intercedes and God changes His mind and decides not to wipe them out (v. 14). (I know it messes with our view of sovereignty. People have said that God knew that Moses would pray and that He would have mercy. Okay, but the fact that God leaves the part of changing His mind in the Bible means that God must want us to know that He can change His mind. Whatever that means. God hurts my head!) Anyway, in chapter 33, Moses asked to see the glory of the Lord (v. 18). God's response to this request revealed some great truths about the glory. "Then He said, 'I will make all My goodness pass before you, and I will proclaim the name of the Lord before you'" (Exodus 33:19). Moses asked the Lord, "Please show me your glory." And God responded with two things: His goodness and His name.

God's name carries with it all the implications of that name; virtues, characteristics, power, etc. But God sums them all up in one word: *goodness*. The glory of God is the goodness of God. We expect God to be mean, angry, and stern. Historically, mankind all over the world has come to the conclusion, on their own, that the gods must be angry! But Jehovah, Yahweh, the God of Abraham, Isaac, and Jacob is a God who is slow to anger, abounding in love, and filled with mercy, justice, peace, and grace. You see, everyone expects God to be angry with those who have sinned against Him, what is not expected is a God who loves us enough to die for us. What glory!

There is one other way in this passage that God describes His glory. The Lord said, "So it shall be, while My glory passes by, that I will put you in the cleft of the rock, and will cover you with My hand while I pass by" (Exodus 33:22). Do you see it? God's presence is also His glory. Headache yet? Work with me here. God called Himself "I am." This is because He not only performs miraculous works, but whatever He does is a revelation of His nature. He does not simply rescue us from sin; He is the Rescuer. He does not simply heal; He is the ultimate Healer. He does not simply deliver; He is the Deliverer. He does not simply do good, He is the ultimate good.

The Great Attribute Theory

I have this theory. I call it the Great Attribute theory. God has many attributes, like mercy, love, sovereignty, etc. My theory goes like this: any attribute that God has, He must be the ultimate and greatest expression of that attribute. For example: if He is good, then He must be the best at being good, the ultimate expression. If He is love, then He must give the highest and greatest love. If God says He is something (attribute), then He must be the best at it, not because His ego cannot handle anyone being better, but because everyone else was created by Him and is thus subservient to Him. If God is love, then there is no one who can love better than God, or they would be superior to God in the area of love.

A mother's capacity to love was created by God. This brings a whole new level of complications into view. When my parents tell me they love me, I can understand what that means; they want the best for me, to protect me, to care for me. But with some people's theology, when God says He loves them, it means He may make them sick, hurt them tragically to teach a lesson, or take away a loved one because He is mad. How is it that I can understand my mother when she says she loves me, but not understand God when He says it? Could we be wrong about God? You may ask, "Could you be wrong about your mother's love?" Yes, I am sure that happens, but in this case Romans 13:10 says, "Love does no harm to a neighbor." The word *harm* in the original language means to cause distress, injury, even to make ill.

If the above scenario is true, then when God says He loves me, He could mean He hates me, or He could mean He wants to kill me. With this theology, there is no grid for understanding God when He communicates one of His deepest virtues, love! Because God is love, He loves me better than my mother ever could, and I can know what that love looks like, because He demonstrated it in Christ on the cross.

To sum up this thought: God, who is all-powerful and has every legitimate right to send me to hell with the demons and the devil, chooses to love me, die for me, enter covenant with me, bless me, be good to me. Why? Because it is who He is…good! Praise the glory of His grace!

Reduced to Strength

The enemy has moved in close to attack Israel and Gideon has blown the trumpet and rallied the troops. In Judges 7:2, we find God has a problem with this situation, "The people who are with you are too many for Me to give the Midianites into their hands, lest Israel claim glory for itself against Me, saying, 'My own hand has saved me.'" The Israelites will not conquer the enemy, God will give the enemy over to them. It did not matter if they had fifty thousand men or two men; the victory was going to be because of God. And God wanted to make sure that Israel understood that. So He reduced them to a place of complete dependence on Him.

The issue with God is His glory, so He removes certain men and chooses other men. I would like to look at what God removes and what God chooses, for what He removes would have contributed to stealing glory. So, it would be good to remove those things from our lives. Furthermore, if we can understand why God chose the men He did, we can cultivate those things in our lives to keep the glory in the right place. So, let's look…

First, God sent home those who where fearful and afraid (Judges 7:3). In our journey to renewal, fear has come up once again. The Lord is really after obliterating fear from our hearts. Fear causes us to shrink back from giving, serving, worshiping, or obeying. Psalms 37:8 (NIV) says, "Do not fret—it only leads to sin." Proverbs 29:25 tells us, "The fear of man (what they think of us or what they might do to us) brings a snare, but whoever trusts in the Lord shall be safe." Notice fear verses trust. Jesus asked His fearful disciples, "How is that you have no faith?" (Mark 4:40).

Fear is the opposite of faith. We either walk in fear or faith. Unhealthy fear is grounded in surviving, in self-centeredness, in being self-aware, whereas faith rests in surrender, in being God-centered, in being God-aware. Fear makes us unstable. My grandpa was a coon hunter. He knew quite a bit about dogs, or it appeared he did. Once I was with him and some of his buddies and their dogs. As

I was petting the dogs, some were disobedient and jumping on me. I was young and these dogs were big, so it wasn't like they needed to get down off my knees—it was more like they needed to get off my shoulders and out of my face. I came to this one dog and reached out to pet him. He looked calm and cool, but as I reached out my hand, Grandpa grabbed me and said, "No, Hoss, you don't wanna mess with him." Being young, I naturally asked, "Why?" He answered, "A disobedient dog is better than a scared dog. That dog looks all right, but he ain't. He's afraid, and you never know what a scared dog like that is going to do." And much like a coon dog, when we are scared, we are unstable, and God knew that fear would cause men to be unstable and take the glory for themselves. For renewal to come, we must fear the Lord only.

In Judges 7:4–7 we find:

> But the Lord said to Gideon, "The people you have are still too many; bring them down to the water, and I will test them for you there. Then it will be, that of whom I say to you, 'This one shall go with you,' the same shall go with you; and of whomever I say to you, "This one shall not go with you," the same shall not go. So he (Gideon) brought the people down to the water. And the Lord said to Gideon, "Everyone who laps from the water with his tongue, as a dog laps, you shall set apart by himself; likewise everyone who gets down on his knees to drink." And the number of those who lapped, putting their hand to their mouth, was three hundred men; but all the rest of the people got down on their knees to drink water. Then the Lord said to Gideon, "By the three hundred men who lapped I will save you, and deliver the Midianites into your hand."

God chose men that drew the water to their mouth to take a drink. This communicated two things: first, God chose those who stayed aware, and second, he did not chose the others who were distracted by their flesh. Let's look at how I came to these conclusions.

Bringing the water to your mouth was a way of drinking and

still keeping watch for the enemy. God chose people who were aware of the enemy, aware of the war, and aware of the assignment. There are many Christians who live completely oblivious to the reality that there is a devil who hates them. There are some who have created an idea of God's sovereignty that makes rebuking the devil somehow opposition to God's will. Meaning, if God is controlling everything, then there is no need to rebuke the devil, right?

Furthermore, there are many who are not walking in awareness of the kingdom of God and how, at any minute, God can be orchestrating a kingdom visitation. It could be with the waiter, on the phone, or while working with people. A person normally sees what they are looking for. So, be aware and look for the presence of God to lead you everywhere.

Ephesians 6:18 gives us insight into how the New Testament believer stays aware. "Praying always with all prayer and supplication in the Spirit, being watchful…" Constant prayer in our spirit is the equivalent of bringing the water to your mouth to drink. Unceasing prayer in our spirit keeps us watchful, ready, and aware. Many people are not used by God, because they simply are not looking for Him to speak. Paul said, "You are not restricted by us, but you are restricted by your own affections" (2 Corinthians 6:12), Many Christians do not turn their affections to God when they walk into the supermarket, so they cannot hear or see what He is doing there.

This is a big deal. If God is going to be our strength then constant reliance on Him should be our highest objective. Basically, if He is our greatest strength, then anything that distracts us from depending on Him is our greatest weakness—whether it be tradition, formula, talents, appearances, our own strengths, etc. Anything that distracts us from dependence on Him is destructive.

This leads me to the second point. In choosing one type of drinker, God excluded the other. Why? Well, if we go back to the beginning of Judges 7, we catch an important piece of information. The group of men following Gideon traveled from Ophrah to Harod. This is approximately nine to fifteen miles in a Middle

Eastern climate. Then God took them down to the well to give them something to drink. Those who drank like dogs probably did not always do that (let's hope). They were probably extremely thirsty. The men who brought the water up to their mouths maintained awareness in spite of the thirst. Conversely, God did not choose those who were distracted from their assignment by the desires of their flesh.

When I say "desire of the flesh," I do not mean a lust, even though certainly there are people distracted from the purposes of God by sinful lusts. However, God is testing the men, and He does not test with sin. A temptation to sin is not a test from God (James 1:13). What I am talking about is simply being distracted by thirst, a normal need. This is the point: one group satisfied a basic need while keeping their focus on the assignment, while the other was absorbed with and distracted by meeting their immediate physical need. Jesus said it this way, "But seek first the kingdom of God and His righteousness, and all these things shall be added to you" (Matthew 6:33). It is not always the big sins that can distract us, but little things like paying the bills, food to eat, our jobs, and the daily grind of life. Seeking the satisfying of a basic need, we can lose sight of Him and become unstable and risk placing the glory in the wrong place—us!

Reducing the Strength of a Leader

Briefly, I would like to look at how God dealt with fear in Gideon. In Judges 7:3, God gave the option of going home to anyone who was fearful or afraid—22,000 people went home! But in verse 10, God said to Gideon, "But if you are afraid, go down to the camp (that's the enemy's camp) with Purah your servant..." God told the followers when they were afraid they could go home, but told the leader to go closer to the enemy. Leaders do not always have the same options as followers.

We later read, "Then he (Gideon) went down with Purah" (v. 11). You know Purah had be saying, "Thanks for bringing me up God." Anyway, they went down to the enemy's camp and heard one soldier tell the other about a dream he had. The other soldier interprets the dream as being "nothing else but the sword of Gideon."

The Bible tells, in verse 15, that Gideon worshiped. I do not think Gideon worshiped because he finally realized that he could win this war but rather realized the depth of his unbelief (faulty belief system, or bad theology) and how patient God had been with Him. He had thought that God had forsaken him, argued with God about his qualifications for leadership, went at night to tear down his father's idols because he was afraid, and tested God—not once but twice—with the fleece. He worshiped because He had a glimpse of God's nature. He worshiped because it was the only proper response to the revelation he had of the goodness of God!

Pruning the Pathway to Fruitfulness

The strength of Israel was not in her numbers but in her God. God removed false strengths to produce complete dependence so He could give them their enemy. This Old Testament action is what the New Testament calls pruning. Jesus said, "I am the true vine, and My Father is the vinedresser. Every branch in Me that does not bear fruit He takes away; and every branch that bears fruit He prunes, that it may bear more fruit" (John 15:1–2). Pruning is Father God reducing us to our core strength, reducing us to abiding in and depending on Him.

Growth starts with subtraction. Every Christian is going through pruning, has recently come out of a pruning, or is about to go into a season of pruning. If you are in a season of fruitfulness, it is because you survived last season's pruning. If we are planning on moving on, we must enter another season of pruning. In a season where we resist the Father's pruning, we level off and stop growing (we become a camper). Times of pruning are not always fun and are rarely pleasant, but it must be what we as Christians desire, because we want to grow to bear fruit. We trust the Father's gardening skills and surrender to them. And although it is uncomfortable, we keep in mind the fruit that we will bear and how it will bring Him glory! Trusting Him to cut away the bad things and leave the good positions us to give Him glory when there is fruit. Pruning positions us to place the glory in the correct person!

SWEET RELEASE

The horse is prepared for the day of battle, but the deliverance is
of the Lord.

Proverbs 21:31

God is really good at winning. However, He fights battles in the some
peculiar ways. He walks around walls and blows a trumpet; He parts a
sea for His people and then lures the enemy into it and drowns them.
And with Gideon, He orders three hundred men at night to "sneak
up" on the enemy with torches and trumpets. And to ensure the ele-
ment of surprise, He wants them to blow their trumpets.

Before all that takes place, God gives Gideon some confirma-
tion through a dream of the enemy (Judges 7:13–15). The interpretation caused Gideon to worship. This word *worship* means to bow.
This is the first lesson in how to let God fight your battles: submit.
Bring any area of your life that is not in submission to God under
His reign. I am a firm believer that a man will never reach a place
of victory when he has not been in worship. Worship must be the
starting place. I am not talking about the singing time in our services, I am talking about applying the right worth to the right person. The Holy Spirit is to have the proper place in our lives. He is
worthy of our complete submission. Anything less will not do.

Next, Gideon commanded the people to *arise*. There is a lot said in that single word. Arise, change your position. Get up! Stand to your feet. Something has just taken place that demands we move from sitting or relaxing to a position of advancement. In order for reformation to come to the evangelical community, the saints will have to arise. We will have to change our position, from one of comfort to one of readiness. It is pretty obvious that the one we have had is not working.

Then Gideon simply repeated what God had told him through the interpretation of the enemy's dream. "Arise, for the Lord has delivered the camp of Midian into your hand" (Judges 7:15). There is a vast multiplicity of opinions about the Word of Faith movement. I have read enough to be familiar with the principle, and do not wish to debate the theology behind it here. However, I would like to simply say this: when it comes down to war time, you better be saying what God is saying or you will be in opposition to His will. Confess what He has said concerning your situation. This is how Jesus overcame Satan in the wilderness! If you want to let God fight your battles, then confess what His Word says about your situation, regardless of what anything else tells you.

"Then he divided the three hundred men into three companies, and he put a trumpet into every man's hand, with empty pitchers, and torches inside the pitchers. And he said to them, 'Look at me and do likewise" (Judges 7:16–17). Gideon organized the men he had and equipped them, but one phrase has always leapt out at me: "do likewise." I believe this is true discipleship (i.e. taking someone and teaching them to do likewise). The church has functioned for some years as an institution instead of a family. I have a degree, in which I took a pastoral counseling class, from a professor who had never been a pastor. This proves how an institution can place principles above performance. This professor, who taught many good things, could only impart principles because he never experienced counseling class from a professor.

The church must return to functioning like a family. If you want to be an evangelist, then find someone in your church who has that gift and hang around him. I have heard it said that there are at least four other people in the Bible who killed giants, and all of them followed David. Bill Johnson has said, "If you want to kill giants, hang out with giant killers." We cannot reduce God down to forms and formulas! We must stop being Israel in Exodus 19, choosing rules over relationship!

Finding the Place of Risk

After Gideon had organized and equipped, he moved into position. "So Gideon and the hundred men who were with him came to the outpost of the camp" (Judges 7:19). This may not seem like a significant verse but it was quite an act of faith. To our knowledge, the men have no "normal" weapon of warfare and are extremely outnumbered, but they followed Gideon all the way up to the edge of the enemy's camp. That is no easy task.

John Wimber said, "You spell faith, R-I-S-K." I encourage people to find that place where it takes risk to obey God and live there. I am not advising anyone to be stupid. Jesus said, "The world will see Me no more, but you will see Me. Because I live, you will live also" (John 14:19). This verse gives us some key insights into seeing God move in our lives. Suppose Siamese twins shared a heart. One body held the heart; the other did not, but shared his brother's. The one with the heart could say to other, "Because I live, you also live. In essence, your life depends on me." Jesus is saying that as we live dependent on Him, we will see Him show up. If you are not seeing God move, then become more dependent on Him. Find that place of risk where, if He does not show up, you have blown it big.

Longevity

The last insight we draw from this story on how to let God fight your battles is found in Judges 7:21: "And every man stood in his place all around the camp." They stood. The Bible teaches us that when you have done all to stand, stand still. This is a great sign of faith. Faith is not determined by whether or not God did it the first time, but being confident that He is faithful to perform His promise, you stand. If good is going to overcome evil, we have to be committed to the long-term. It may take time for our churches and denominations to find release from the collapse, but give it time.

This will challenge our ability to trust Him. Psalm 37:5 gives us a revelation into how to trust, "Commit your way to the Lord, Trust also in Him, And He shall bring it to pass." Trusting God comes from committing things to God. Paul said it this way, "For I know who I have believed in and am persuaded that He is able to keep (trust) what I have committed to Him until that day" (2 Timothy 1:12). Paul could trust the Lord as a result of a lifetime of committing. Keep committing your life and situations to Jesus and trust will be produced. Trusting is the result of committing.

When God brings this coming reformation, it will be far bigger and better than anything we could imagine or build. It will be beautiful and orderly. It will reach the world and touch the nations. His kingdom will come in such a way that the present days of drought and hopelessness will be turned into days of rejoicing and increase.

Gideon submitted through worship, the men changed their stance—confessed what God was saying, led by example, acted in faith, and committed to stand in their place—and God won the battle. Three hundred men defeated hundreds of thousands through complete reliance on God. Our job is to prepare the horse for battle (an act of faith), and God brings the deliverance. Paul commanded Timothy to "fight the good fight of faith" (1 Timothy 6:12). Our fight is to maintain faith and reliance in God; His part is to perform His promises.

The Fruit of the Kingdom

. . . and the country was quiet for forty years . . .

Judges 8:28

This one verse reveals so much. For forty years the people of God enjoyed peace. The fruit of the kingdom is filled with peace, joy, righteousness, justice, and increase, but most of all, when the kingdom of God comes, it satisfies. When God's manifested presence comes and displays the kingdom, it causes our hearts to be overwhelmed. Because when the Christian sees the kingdom of God enacted, the Christian will realize that he or she was born for this. Seeing the kingdom come will bring reformation, but more importantly, it envelops the hearts of saints and causes passion to arise, because that is the very thing for which we were created.

When God commands us to seek first the kingdom of God, He knows that it will satisfy. Jesus taught that the Father takes pleasure in giving the kingdom to us (Luke 12:32). He was reinforcing what David said, "You (God) open Your hand and satisfy the desire of every living thing" (Psalm 145:16). God gives us the kingdom and the kingdom satisfies. What a glorious and gracious God!

The Need for Longevity

Reform has come many times in the history of the church. However, I do not think that is God's will. Having multiple reformations means that the church did not continue on with the Lord, and we see Israel with the same problem.

So it was, as soon as Gideon was dead, that the children of Israel again played the harlot with the Baals . . . Thus the children of

> Israel did not remember the Lord their God, who had delivered
> them from the hands of all their enemies.
>
> Judges 8:33–34

As soon as the leader died, the people went back to their old ways. There is a reason for this. There is a way to make sure that this does not happen. We must learn how to connect generations to ensure that what God does in someone is built upon in the next generation, not having to start all over again. As has been said, "One generation's ceiling should be the next generation's floor." How do we make that a reality? That is our next subject…

part 3

WALKING IN RESURRECTED LIFE:

CREATING A KINGDOM CULTURE

CULTURE

Movements to Monuments

Have you ever felt cheated when it came to your Christian experience? Ever feel like you signed up for a revolution but got religion? Christianity was meant to be a movement. However, instead of continuing the movement that Jesus and the great cloud of witness handed us, we have made monuments to them. We have, out of a false sense of honor, dishonored God and those who have gone before us. However, God stands ready to forgive and the great cloud of witnesses stands waiting to see us run our part.

A movement begins when a thought is birthed into a reality; a movement is feet for a thought. A movement, good or bad, must have a culture to sustain itself. The disciples of occult have a culture, Mormons have a culture, Amish have a culture, the church has a culture, countries have cultures, etc. Many schools of thought that have no intellectual or factual grounding are still alive because a culture was created to sustain that movement. Some movements that were true and noble have suffered great loss because a culture was not created.

A culture is a people's *norm*—their traditions, worldview, paradigm, and most importantly their core values. The word *culture* could be synonymous with paradigm. A paradigm is a way of thinking. A paradigm is the *why* of the thoughts. For example, we have all met a person that always sees the negative. We ask why this person thinks that way. The answer is inside that person's paradigm. It is the lens that determines how a person views reality. In Luke 8:18, Jesus said, "Be careful how you hear…" He was not talking about being careful of what you hear, but how you hear. A paradigm has the greatest effect on *how* a person hears, but the greatest contributor to a person's paradigm (culture) is that person's core values.

The Heart of the Matter

The Bible says that where our treasure (or value) is, there our heart will be also (Luke 13:34). This verse gives us key insight: what we value reveals our heart. Things highly valued are those which a person will sacrifice to have, whereas core values are things they are willing to die for. Every person has high values and core values. I am writing this portion of this chapter while I am in India. I am visiting an orphanage that our church has partnered with. On this trip, I have discovered some things that I highly value: I highly value a toilet (better yet, a clean toilet). I spent six hours on a train that had a hole cut in the floor. I love a good challenge. Second, I highly value air conditioning. Third, beef! However, I have also discovered some of my core values. First, while walking through a crowded Bapatla street, I was prepared to do whatever it cost to protect my wife and those with me—a core value. Second, I realized that visiting India could possibly pose a threat to my life (the Mumbai terrorist attacks had recently taken place). However, I sensed that the Lord told me to go—another core value.

Core values help make up our hearts. A young woman's core values will determine whether or not she will sleep with a boyfriend years before she is in that situation. Our core values determine how we will react long before we are confronted with a situation. In fact, all behavioral issues are issues of the heart. Many people try to manipulate good behavior from the outside in (which is an Old Testament principal), but if you can rectify the heart you will rectify the behavior. Jesus said, "If you love me you will keep my commandments" (John 14:15). From an Old Testament viewpoint Jesus is saying, "If you really loved me, you would do what I say. So, I'm takin' my toys home!" However, from a New Testament viewpoint Jesus could be saying, "If you focus on loving (or valuing) me, then your natural response will be obedience." People who feel like they have to put the shoulder to the grindstone to obey God need to let God change their core values. Holiness was meant to be lived out of love not law.

Jesus said that the kingdom of heaven is within you (Luke 17:21). I believe He was saying that all kingdom issues are issues that derive from the heart. God is after our hearts—not simply part of our affections, but the full focus of our hearts. He did say, "Love Me with all your heart…" A kingdom is a king's domain, his rulership, his reign. God wants to reign in us, but He does not do so by force or by violently overpowering us in a tyrannical way. He wants to capture our hearts. God will not overpower us until we submit to His Lordship. At least not yet—that is reserved for when He returns. For now He intends to win us over with His love.

We create a culture, or maybe are birthed into one, in which we become comfortable and we fight to protect those comforts. We fight against what makes us uncomfortable and celebrate when everything goes according to our plan. That's not evil, just human. We celebrate regardless of whether our plans were from God or not. Man comes up with a perspective that makes sense to him and brings him pleasure. Eventually, perspectives can become traditions and traditions, cultures.

Most church cultures become closed to input, because all that matters is protecting what is valuable to that culture, without questioning if its values or traditions are of the kingdom. Many churches have valued things that God has not communicated value in. Furthermore, one can develop a tradition or culture around something

God said in the past; then fights to protect that tradition, at the expense of moving forward with Him. Remember, if Abraham would have done what God had said at the expense of what God was saying, he would have been guilty of killing his future. When people refuse to continue on with God, they are by default choosing to camp; in doing so, they are choosing where to die. Sometimes we create a theology of compromise by lowering Scripture to make us feel comfortable with our present spiritual death. Instead of repenting and adjusting to His presence, many choose to stay ignorant and continue to compromise while sweeping other issues under the mysterious "rug" of sovereignty.

People can love their traditions to the point of becoming stubborn. In 1 Samuel 15:23, it says that stubbornness is as iniquity and idolatry. Stubbornness is as idolatry because value is placed upon the will of the person above the will of God. Many cultures, out of their stubbornness, create classes on how to guard and protect traditions. Some seminaries are institutions that teach people how to protect their doctrine. They teach people the way to make the same mistake for centuries. Most of our traditions and cultures are backward from God's. Saul (who later became Paul) had traditions that enabled him to believe that killing innocent people was pleasing to God—the same God who sent Jesus into the world to die for those people because He loved the world. How backwards! Saul thought he had God's heart and values but he was clearly deceived.

Reformation: Our Need but Not Always Our Want

When God brings revival or reformation He brings what we need but not always what we want. What we need might actually offend us. The Israelites were looking for the Messiah that would restore the kingdom to Israel, One that would kick the mean old Romans out of their land. But God sent them a Savior, which is what they needed. They were looking for a conquering king and God sent that King as a child born in a manger. Traditionally, kings are not born in stalls, but God counteracted their tradition.

In the reformation, God countered the church's traditions through Martin Luther. God gave what was needed, and what was needed came in the form of theology. The Reformation was a return to the inerrancy of Scripture. Martin Luther challenged his culture's traditions and therefore suffered persecution. However, today we reap the benefits of such a countercultural reformation. In the Great Awakening, God used John Wesley and George Whitfield to bring a revival that took on a different look than the Reformation. This movement of God exhibited open-air preaching, thousands coming to Christ, and all sorts of different manifestations—shaking, falling, and visions. (John Wesley actually had to start ministering through open-air preaching because he was not allowed in churches; he challenged their traditions.)

So we see that revival and reformation can take on many different faces. We must not reduce it down to one certain experience. We are to cry out to God and receive His response however it comes. God created each human alike yet vastly different. This same God, who is infinitely creative, can pour revival out and bring reformation in many different ways. We must allow Him the freedom to be Himself. What He brings will be what we need, and the outcome will always be the same: God capturing the hearts and possessing the entirety of a person.

Is This God?

When God shows up in our midst, it will counteract our traditions. When He does, we might ask, "Is this God?" We may argue that the reason we ask is that we want the authentic. However, if we really were concerned about the authentic, why did we not ask if our "normal" was of God? For example: someone dances in a worship service (in a culture where that is not normal), and a person asks, "Is that of God, or are they just doing that because it makes them *feel* good?" Why does that person, who asks if this of God, not look at the person who sits quietly in their seat week after week doing nothing and ask, "Is that God, or are they just doing that because it makes them *feel* good?" If you look at the Scriptures, you might find more proof of worship being dramatic then you would of it being quiet and still. Could we really be asking, "Is this God because He did not check with me to see if doing this would make me uncomfortable?"

A closed culture only challenges or questions something that challenges the norm. An open culture does not challenge anything, but we are to be a clear-minded culture. If our core values are not God's, then they will be threatened when He shows up. If we value what He does, they will not. If the present church culture values comfort, smooth services, and intellect, then when God shows up making us uncomfortable, making a mess of our services, and does not bother to explain Himself, our culture will experience turbulence.

Things Sacred

Every tradition has its sacred things. Many different things can become sacred. Many work to guard what is sacred. The only problem is many of our "sacred" things are not sacred to God—buildings, a piano, style of music, rooms in a building, trees, statues, services, etc. When these "sacred" things are not sacred to God, then we are placing value on something He is not. These sacred things, in order to be sacred, have our affections wrapped in them. If our affections are not involved, it is not sacred.

God wants all of us. He is first and foremost after our hearts. Our hearts include our affections. So, if we have some of our affections invested in something sacred that He does not consider sacred then when He shows up wanting our affections it will counter or threaten what is sacred to us. Often times when this happens, we become offended and presume that this cannot be God; He loves my sacred cow! Or this cannot be God; He is the one who made my sacred cow.

God comes along and says, "Gather all the people together in a sacred assembly. I want to meet with my people." So, we gather together in this tent. We experience God in wonderful ways. He shows up and does wonderful things. Because of all the wonderful moments with God in the tent, the tent begins to hold meaning, value. The tent reminds us of the memories, and the memories are precious. That is fine. It is okay to have memories. However, if those memories cause me to be more affectionate toward the tent than I am of the God who encounters me in the tent, then I have entered into idolatry. God values relationship and uses things like a tent as a means to relationship. But often we will sacrifice relationship to obtain, keep, or protect things. This is evidence of idolatry.

The tent was not sacred to God; however, the assembly of people was. The tent was a means to an end. God having relationship with the people, having their affections was the end God was after. The people created something sacred to them that was not sacred to God. So, when He comes to capture their affections back what might He do? He will probably counter their traditions by tearing down their idols, their sacred things, the things that have stolen their affections away from Him.

Many hold the Bible to be sacred in a way never intended by God. In order to somehow protect the greatness and richness of the Scriptures, many have made the experiences in the pages sacred. Some may conclude that the things in the Scriptures are only for certain people, and those certain people are no longer alive. By coming to that conclusion we make the Bible sacred in a way that was never intended by God. For example, in the book of Acts, almost every chapter contains some sort of supernatural communication between God and His people—angels, visions, dreams, etc. If a culture has this wrong view and someone in our church is visited by an angel, has a vision, or a dream they know to be of God, our view of the Bible is threatened. Plus, it makes us uncomfortable knowing someone else has had an experience that I have not. (This is because this person values experience more than the God who initiates the experience.)

Others make the Bible sacred by believing it to be the only way God speaks. However, Jesus said as He was leaving, "I will send the Comforter," not "I will send the Scriptures." Many have made the Scriptures the fourth member of the Godhead—or worse yet, replaced the third member with the Scriptures and made it the Father, Son, and Holy Bible. It is the nature of religion to want written rules instead of wonderful relationship. God wants intimacy! If you know the Bible more intimately than you know the person Jesus, you have settled short at best or committed idolatry at worst.

The Bible is sacred. However, if we changed our paradigm about *how* or *why* the Scriptures are sacred to line up with why God considers them sacred, we might find room for the same experiences. God's Word is sacred because it points us to Him. Every revelation of Scripture is an invitation into experiencing Jesus (John 5). The Bible is sacred because it reveals the nature of our God, invites us into experiencing intimacy with Him, gives us testimonies and promise that He wants to use to tutor our hearts (shape our values).

God told the Israelites that they could not see His form because they would make an idol (Deuteronomy 4:15, 16), but Moses saw God's back (Exodus 33:23). The further we remove idolatry from our hearts, the more He will reveal Himself to us. As stated previously in Part Two, idolatry is valuing anything, in any area of life, more than God. In order to receive more of God, we must adjust our core values to value His presence. We must remove idolatry from our hearts by not stumbling over our man-made traditions, nullifying the Word of God, or replacing His presence with His Word. If we can honestly make Him our treasure, He will have our hearts, and the rest will be beautiful.

What does God value? What core values must we cultivate to continue on in the kingdom? In the remainder of this book we will look to answer this question. I will present truths that must become core values in order to create a culture that can contain and carry revival, which is the normal kingdom life. As you read, remember that these truths are central to creating and sustaining a kingdom culture.

FATHER GOD

The Father's Heart

If you do not know God, then He probably looks a lot like you. For this reason some may have a distorted view of God. I know that I did. Somehow, looking back, I know that I was not taught this in word, but it seems to have climbed into my heart from somewhere else—this idea that "Gawd" is mad and Jesus knows how to calm Him down. I actually thought at one time that Jesus died to save me from "Gawd." Jesus was the longhaired, limp-wristed, easygoing, snack-after-class, all-around-nice Sunday school guy. And "Gawd" was the one in the sanctuary who did not want you to run in church and who you'd better not make mad! But I am learning as I study, pray, and try to walk with God that He is better than I have ever imagined, and He passionately desires intimacy with His sons and daughters. He wanted a family. He had plenty of angels to serve Him, but He wanted sons and daughters. So, He created man in His image and in His likeness. He created man in such a way that only He could satisfy the heart of man. You probably know the rest—Adam and Eve sinned, they are removed from the garden and cursed. But that did not stop the *father* in God. Believe it or not God was not surprised. Grieved, yes, but not surprised. He already had a plan to recapture the hearts and win back the affections of His scattered children.

We see it in Jesus, in how He died to bring many sons to glory (Hebrews 2). Ephesians chapter 1 tells us that it brought God pleasure to adopt us as sons. This is extremely important. We must realize that anyone in Christ is accepted in the beloved. God the Father is pleased with us, in Christ. One question that we can ask to test our acceptance of this revelation is, "Can I sit here and do nothing for Him and realize that He is pleased?" I don't have to preach, witness, pray, or serve for Him to be pleased with me. God is not calling us to do this; but if He did, could we? This is what it means to be accepted, and this should be the posture of the New Testament believer.

Christian, we may not realize it, but sometimes we try to fast, pray, or praise our way into pleasing Him. And all of our works are as filthy rags. One thing that keeps us from receiving His gifts of grace is trying to earn them, which is why the prostitutes and tax collectors could receive Jesus but the Pharisees could not. The Pharisees thought that their works earned them favor, but the prostitute knew she needed grace, and Jesus was ready to give it. God wants to be gracious toward us for the praise of the glory of His grace, but when we try to earn His gracious gifts, it will not be for the praise of grace but because of our working. But if we learn to receive as sons, He will gladly give. For example, say a man is fasting and seeking the Lord for a greater anointing in teaching. The Father wants to pour out a greater anointing on the man, but He knows that it will only distract the man from Him (and the Father is the best thing for the man). So, Father God withholds this gift even though He wants to give it. However, if this same man rests in God's grace, realizing that God is happy with him in Christ, then he is positioned to receive the gift because the gift will no longer distract the man from the Father; the man will not find his value in the anointing, because he found it in his Father.

In Ezekiel 44:18, God, speaking of the priest who were to minister before Him, instructs, "They shall not clothe themselves with anything that causes sweat." Why sweat? It is the residue of man's labor. God is saying that those who will minister to Him must be grounded in the fact they are before Him by His grace, not by their efforts. I believe this is what it means to be "established in the faith" (Colossians 2:6,7), to be set in faith alone. Everything in the kingdom is received by faith; nothing is earned. When the writer of Hebrews said, "He who enters His rest has ceased from his works," he meant it. Rest in Him or work to please Him, but a man cannot do both.

Jesus is our only hope of pleasing the Father. God cannot become more pleased with Christ, and our lives are hidden in Christ, therefore He cannot become more pleased with me. This is what it means to have become the "righteousness of Christ" (2 Corinthians 5:21). From this position of trusting in the finished work of Christ, New Testament ministry begins and ends. Jesus did not start his ministry until after he heard, "This is my beloved son, in whom I am well pleased."

We have nothing that can possibly come close to repaying God for all He has done. The psalmist states, "How shall I repay the Lord for all his benefits? I will drink of the cup of salvation and call upon the name of the Lord" (Psalm 116:12). We cannot repay him, but we can and should enjoy the gift. When a dad gives a gift to his son he is most honored when his son enjoys the gift, but not so much when his son tries to pay it back. Servants earn wages, but sons receive inheritances.

Trying to earn or repay God for grace actually degrades it. "Now to him who works, the wages are not counted as grace but as debt" (Romans 4:4). What can we really add to the finished work of Christ? If God is not pleased with us in Christ, after all Christ has done, then none of our works are going to add anything. Many Christians are trying to pay God back for salvation; but if you pay God back for grace, it ceases to be grace. However, enjoying, embracing, and walking in the fullness of grace is honoring to the Giver of Grace and the One who paid the bill.

Peter tells us to "grow in the grace and knowledge of our Lord Jesus" (2 Peter 3:8). I believe that the more value we put in the grace of God the more we grow in grace and the more we mature! Jesus, who fully pleased God, still grew in favor with God (Luke 2:52). The more we value grace, enjoy grace, dance in grace, praise the glory of His grace, the more we will grow in favor with God! Righteousness is a gift; receive it by faith (Romans 5:17).

The Father's Love and Sin

And Jesus said to her, "Neither do I condemn you; go and sin no more

John 8:11

I believe that we were created to give God pleasure and for Him to be our pleasure. The way I see it, we were created with "buckets" that only God could fill and satisfy (Psalm 145:16). Sin is simply the expression of an empty bucket; it is my attempt to fill these buckets with anything other than God.

Of all of our buckets, a person has a security bucket and a value bucket. When I try to fill my security bucket up with anything besides the Father, I sin. For example, I might try to fill this bucket with material possessions. One might think they are secure when they have a large enough 401k, a better job, a significant other, or a bigger ministry; but this is the sin of idolatry. A man might find his value in his title. As president of a successful company, this man would consider himself valuable. However, as soon as the company declines or goes bankrupt because of recession the man considers himself a failure. And if the man's identity is found in his position, then the man will probably lie to keep it or steal to make his business successful. All of this is sin, because the man's value bucket is not filled with what satisfies, which is God. If the man believes he is valuable because he is a child of the King, then his bucket will be filled, and he will not be as tempted to lie, steal, or cheat.

Let's identify some ways to tell if your buckets are filled with something besides God. First, look at the areas of continued or strong sin. If a person is a habitual liar, look at their reasons for lying. If a person is always lying about how "good" he is, it might be because he thinks his good works will determine his value. He has filled his value bucket up with good works. Or a person might lie about how "bad" he is to appear rebellious or tough. A person who does this could either value being tough or is doing it for security. He might think, *If everyone thinks that I am tough, then I'm safe from them picking on me.*

Second, look at the things in your life that frustrate you. The above person that values the good works (Martha) will be frustrated by people who do not carry their weight and do good too. Because they find their value in good works, they will find others valuable for their good works. This person will be hard to convince that they are wrong because it is easy to say, "I am right, people ought to carry their weight." Aren't you glad God did not act that way to you! I used to be frustrated with ignorant people, people who did not think things out. That is because I valued intelligence. "The smarter you are, the better you are" was my philosophy. So, I would become frustrated with people for their ignorant decisions.

The last two ways of identifying the wrong stuff in your bucket is to answer the following questions with honesty. Is there anything in your life you could not live without? And is there anything you could obtain that would solve all your problems? These questions just scratch the surface, but they will help identify some of the things that we are filling our buckets with that will never truly satisfy.

God wants to satisfy our hearts with Himself, but many might think that God will only satisfy their hearts when they quit sinning. This is the bondage of religion. A person may think (or may have been taught) that God will share intimacy with those who do not sin, but if you think about it, a person needs this intimacy with God in order to refrain from sin. So this person tries to earn God's love and intimacy by not sinning only to find it an impossible task. If this person will repent for trying to please God with his goodness and for filling his buckets with other things, then God will come and empty the buckets and fill the buckets with Himself. With satisfied buckets he will not have to look anywhere else or to anything else to satisfy. I have heard it put this way; whatever truth demands, grace supplies. We all need to hear, "Neither do I condemn you," to be able to go and sin no more! This concept is difficult to the religious mind, because it takes us completely out of the picture. It is God satisfying our hearts through Christ and then Christ living through us. We cannot boast in our works or judge others harshly because it was all Christ in us. It is really all about Him!

This means that all behavior issues are heart issues. God knows that outside manipulation like fear and punishment will not correct the internal problem of the heart. Jesus said, "If you love me, you will keep my commandments" (John 14:15). When we filter this verse through our Old Testament lenses, we hear, "You did that! Well, you really must not love me, I'm taking my toys home!" However, the real meaning may be different. The point He is making is that true obedience is linked to love not to law. Jesus is saying, "If you focus on loving me, you will keep my commandments; trust me!"

The Father's Love: A Key to Obedience

For the Father loves the Son, and shows Him all things that He Himself does …

John 5:20

The key to Jesus's ministry was He did only what He saw the Father doing and said what the Father was saying (John 5:19). What would our churches look like if we only did what He was blessing instead of doing "something" and asking Him to bless it? As we grow in our revelation of our sonship we will learn that the Father loves to show us what He is doing. *For Christians, seeing what the Father is doing and hearing what the Father is saying ought to be as normal as breathing.*

The Father loves His children, and as we grow in our awareness of this love, it will tutor our eyes to see and our ears to hear. He loves His children and desires to show us what He is doing and speak to us. Having our hearts established in the Father's love (a core value) will grow our faith to expect to see what He is doing and hear what He is saying, and quicken our obedience when we do!

First Samuel 15:22 says, "To obey is better than sacrifice." If obedience is better than sacrifice, then it cannot be both! God obviously does not view obedience, any obedience, as a sacrifice. When we view our obedience as a sacrifice we are seeing the situation from our limited perspective and we are functioning from an unrenewed mind. Whatever God calls us to do is the best thing for us! His will is "good, acceptable, and perfect!" (Romans 12:2). Sons who understand the goodness and love of their Father will not see obedience as sacrifice, but the opposite. Disobedience will always be more expensive than obedience.

The Father's Love and Biblical Fear

> But I will show you whom you should fear: Fear Him who, after He has killed, has the power to cast into hell; yes, I say to you, fear Him!....But the very hairs of your head are all numbered. Do not fear therefore; you are of more value than the sparrows.
>
> Luke 12:5–7

I have heard it said that, "You cannot lose through bad works what you did not earn through good works." We all have the same concern that people may take advantage of grace, which will lead to irreverence. Even Paul addressed the same issue. He wrote in Romans 6:1, "What shall we say then? Shall we continue in sin that grace may abound? Certainly not!" I dare say that unless someone has put a disclaimer on grace, they have not taught biblical grace.

God is Jehovah Jireh, Jehovah Nissi, and Jehovah sneaky! After a person tastes grace and is "born again," their nature is changed. 2 Corinthians 5:17 refers to this as a new creation. This new creation has the ability to sin but does not have the ability to enjoy it! A saint is still capable of committing a sin, but it is no longer his occupation.

This brings us to the difference between conviction and condemnation. Condemnation ties sin to a person's identity while conviction ties holiness and righteousness to a person's nature. When a person lies, condemnation says, "You are a liar! You always lie!" Conviction says, "This is not who you are so why are you acting like this?" A Christian actually has to go against their true nature to sin!

When tackling the principles of the Father's love and a healthy fear, there are two truths for us to consider. First, Jesus had a close and intimate relationship with the Father, in which there was no fear of punishment, yet He still feared God. Secondly, when Jesus taught on the fear of the Lord, He mentioned how valuable we are to the Father. Seeing ourselves as valuable to our Father keeps us from unhealthy fears and leads us into a healthy fear of God. Unhealthy fear causes us to shrink back from God, as the Israelites did at Mount Sinai. Healthy fear equips us to walk into the cloud as Moses did on that same mountain. Moses knew his place with God, he knew he had favor, and that enhanced his healthy fear of God. Maybe this will help. Here is an excerpt from one of my journal entries:

Why am I so timid to believe that He could actually be pleased with me? I mean, if he is not pleased with me in Christ then what can I possibly add? How can I please God more with my works if what Christ did didn't please Him? If I don't trust God to be my Savior, then why would I trust Him to be my Judge!!

It's like I am so conditioned to work to please Him that I am afraid that if He is pleased with me then I won't pray, witness, fast, care, or love. But that thought has more faith in punishment than love! It's like I am more convinced that punishment or fear motivates better than love. The only problem with this is that God does not think this way. He actually thinks love cannot fail.

Is the goal God has for us good behavior? Is that what He is ultimately after, getting us to behave correctly? If that was the ultimate goal why give freewill, why not make robots? Could it be that God values relationship more than behavior? It has to be, He died to be with me not because I deserved it through good behavior. Not that behavior is unimportant; it's just not the main thing. Maybe God knows the only way we will behave like Him is Him living through us? Or maybe through relationship with Him, intimacy with Him, He will produce this behavior? But if it's behavior before love, none of us would ever be loved, not to mention we would have earned it.

What has tutored my heart to fear what I will become if He is pleased with me? Why do I assume that if there is no threat of wrath being poured out on me when I do something bad, that I won't love Him? Why can I not just love Him? Why can I not just serve him to serve him? If I only serve Him to avoid His punishment, then I'm serving out of fear, not love. And the great commandment is to love the Lord, not be afraid of the Lord. Not to mention how tyrannical that sounds. Is that really God? It sounds more like Hitler. Have we confused the ways of the devil with the ways of God? I mean even the ways of man over the ways of God is demonic! Hitler used fear and punishment to manipulate behavior, does God? Surely not!

What if the real way God changes us is to have deep meaningful relationship even when we don't act right, even when we don't deserve it and in this display of 'unconditional' love we are conditioned to love Him back? What if He actually overcomes evil, our evil, with His good?!!

The Father's Love and True Worship

> But the hour is coming, and now is, when the true worshiper will worship the Father in spirit and in truth; for the Father is seeking such to worship Him.
>
> John 4:23

When Jesus speaks of the true worshiper he states that true worshipers will worship the *Father* in spirit and in truth. Immediately following this verse, Jesus refers to the Father as "God," stating, "God is spirit." I believe that this is Jesus emphasizing true worship is in the posture of sonship.

To come as Moses did before a holy and righteous God who makes the mountains tremble is an amazing event and would have demanded the highest worship imaginable. Even before that, before He made a covenant with Abraham, delivered the Israelites, or sent Jesus—He deserved our highest worship as Creator God. Our God, Jehovah, did not need worship, but He desired relationship. Our amazing God wanted to have a real relationship with you and me. He wanted a family and has called us His sons. (If you are a lady, it is okay. You work on being a son, and I will work of being a bride.) He deserved all of our worship as Creator, as Deliverer, as Savior … and we did worship Him as such. But He has called us to another level of intimacy: sonship. It is worth noting that Jesus, in His personal walk with the Father, only referred to the Father as "God" when He was forsaken. All of creation—the earth, trees, the ocean, even demons and darkness—will refer to Him as God, but only the redeemed have the privilege to call Him Father.

God called himself "I Am." I believe he was communicating that He does not simply "do" stuff, but that everything He does is a reflection of his nature. He does not only deliver people, He is the Deliverer. He does not only save people, He is the Savior. He could have said, "Moses, all that I am wanting to do through you will be an exact reflection of my nature. Put your hand in your cloak;

now, pull it out. Okay, calm down Moses, put it back in and pull it out again. Yeah, you're going to see some of that—leprosy healed. Why? Because I Am the Healer!" He has given us an invitation into another level of intimacy! When Father God ransomed us and gave us the right to be called sons of God (John 1:12) and sent the spirit of His Son into our hearts to cry out "Abba" (Galatians 4:6), He was saying something about His nature; He desires us to see and worship Him as Father.

The Father's Love: A Key to Prayer and Faith

When you pray say, "Our Father..."

Luke 11:2

Jesus, the only real teacher on prayer and the only one really qualified to teach the subject, starts his teaching with the words "Our Father." Prayer ought to be as simple as a son talking with his loving father. Many try to dive into the depths of prayer while missing the most fundamental aspect of it: a good Father speaks to His children. When we begin to see our sonship and embrace our "Abba" or "daddy," prayer begins to be fun!

A dad who never speaks with his children is a dysfunctional father. When we step into our sonship, we realize it is normal for Father God to speak and for His children to hear. And then the prayer journey can begin. He actually is more willing to speak than many sons are to hear.

Later in the same chapter of Luke mentioned above, Jesus says, "If you then being evil know how to give good gifts to your children, how much more will your Father in heaven give the Holy Spirit to them that ask?" (Luke 11:13). Matthew's version of this verse says, "... how much more will your Father who is in heaven give good things to those that ask Him?" (Matthew 7:11). Jesus was trying to help us understand the goodness of God by comparison. Earthly fathers can give good gifts. If a son asks for bread, the earthly father will not give him a stone. God says that kind of giving comes from a father who is evil. How much more will God give us the Holy Spirit or "good things?" Faith is grounded in knowing our relationship with God as Father. Faith is simply judging the character, Word, and goodness of God correctly. Unbelief arises when I judge the character, Word, and goodness of God incorrectly.

When I pray for a healing or a provision I am not asking a God who is cold and distant. I am asking my loving Father, who gladly gave His only Son to purchase me when I was His enemy. If this extravagant Father did not withhold His only Son, why would he withhold any lesser gift?

The Father's Love:
A Key to Unity

Behold, how good and pleasant it is for brothers to dwell together in unity.

Psalm 133:1

In a time of denominationalism, Christianity could use a good revelation of unity. The Father's love is the answer to division. Notice how good and pleasant it is for "brothers" to dwell together in unity. Family is the key to unity. Denominations are groups of sons and daughters gathered around certain truths, but if we would gather around our Father and not truths, then we could have unity without sacrificing or compromising our beliefs.

I have two sisters, and we do not always see eye to eye. Anybody with siblings will know what I mean. However, we are still in unity because we are a family. Is our Father God and His family not stronger than the division our "beliefs" cause? What if we chose to celebrate the grace that brought us into the family rather than focusing on the beliefs that separate us? Is the Father's love strong enough and wide enough for a charismatic and an evangelical to be family? Could a Baptist worship with a Methodist, or a "tongues-talker" next to a cessationalist? What about a Calvinist alongside an Arminian? This is the heart of our Father: for brothers to live and remain in unity.

Many Christians cling to their particular truths at the sacrifice of unconditional love. The problem is that God said, "He who abides in love abides in God" (1 John 4:16). Bill Johnson said it this way: "Maturity is not seen in truth but in love." Two believers have different views on drinking. One Christian takes a vow of abstinence and decides never to drink alcohol while another brother drinks beer in moderation, never becoming drunk. The Bible may support both views. Maturity is not seen in abstinence or responsibility but in how each man will love the other. I like to put it this way: maturity is not seen in the truth you hold, but the unconditional love you show.

When all denominations have a revelation of sonship, true unity will become possible. We will realize that we did not obtain salvation by our theology or become sons because of our doctrinal statements. But as we see the Father's love for all of His children, we might just find that God is not Calvinist or Arminian, neither is He Baptist or Lutheran, but He is a Father who loves all His children!

From Servants to Sons

> So, he answered and said to his father, "Lo, these many years I have been serving you … yet you never gave me a young goat …"
>
> Luke 15:29

In the parable of the prodigal son, we tend to put our emphasis on the wayward son. However, I would like to suggest the central character in this story is the father. The prodigal son is filled with rebellion and finds himself in a distant land working for others while his brother is home, filled with religion, working for his father. Both sons are working! The prodigal son wastes his inheritance, while the brother cannot receive his because he is trying to earn it.

As soon as the prodigal son returned home the gracious father ran out to greet him. The father celebrated the son's return. And when the older brother was too proud to come in, the gracious father went out to meet with him also. The father wanted the older brother to come in and celebrate. The older brother in the field was trying to earn a goat for his friends, but the father reminded him, "All I have is yours."

Which one are you? The prodigal in the foreign land or the brother trying to earn the father's love? Maybe you are already in the house celebrating with the father. Good; that is right where the father wants you. Both sons in this parable, and many Christians today, need to come out of the servant's quarters and into the Father's house … from servants to sons. This does not mean sons never serve, but that when they do, they realize that they are sons who choose to serve because of the love they have for the Father.

Every revelation from Scripture is an invitation to encounter God. It is our responsibility to put a demand on a revelation until we experience it in our lives. We must pursue the Father while he is pursuing us. We must not let go of the revelation of the heart the Father has for us. We must repent of trying to earn His love, and then ask and keep asking for an encounter with the Father's love. The Bible states we are, "to know the love of Christ which passes knowledge" (Ephesians 3:19). How are we to know something that passes knowledge? We experience it! A person can experience the Father's love even though it makes no sense in his head! We must pursue an encounter with the Father's heart! Never put stipulations on what that encounter ought to look like. My experience does not have to match your experience, but the outcome will be the same. When we encounter this love and are satisfied by it, we will love the Father and all our siblings unconditionally. He is more ready to give us this experience than we might think. The revelation of God as Father and us as His sons must become a core value to create a kingdom culture.

Father, give us a revelation of our sonship and your Father heart. May we repent for trying to add to the work of Christ or pay you back for grace. Oh, what arrogance! Of these things I repent! Father, my heart rejoices in the fact that you are pleased with me in Christ. I come out of the servants' quarters and into Your house, and I behold what manner of love You, my Father, have lavished on me, that I might be called your son! Thank you, Father. Amen!

TRUTH, LIFE, AND REVELATION

The thief does not come except to steal, and to kill, and to destroy. I have come that they may have life, and that they may have it more abundantly.

John 10:10

This is the cosmic conflict—life versus death, darkness versus light. Everything of the kingdom of darkness leads to death. Everything of the kingdom of God leads to life. This "life" that Jesus desires to give is a glorious, victorious, righteous, eternal, abundantly great God life.

"For this purpose the Son of God was manifested that He might destroy the works of the devil" (1 John 3:8b). Everything Jesus did was to destroy the devil and death. Jesus died to put death to death (1 Corinthians 15:55)! The result is resurrected life to all who would believe. This is what Paul referred to in Romans 6 when he said, "newness of life" and in Romans 8:11b, "He who raised Christ from the dead will also give life to your mortal bodies through His Spirit who dwells in you."

Jesus endured the cross; He did not enjoy it. He endured it, because in doing so, He could bring life to many. Paul in Romans 6 argues that if we are "in Christ," then we are in his death (cross) and in His resurrection (life). Jesus did not stay at the cross and neither should we. The reason the cross is power to those who believe is because the cross points to the resurrection. Christians must move to the other side of the cross and into the resurrection. We have died in Christ. Therefore, Paul commands to "reckon" ourselves dead. Many are trying to 'die daily;' however, to 'die daily' means that everyday we should "reckon" ourselves dead. You do not have to kill your old man today, but "reckon," consider, meditate, on the reality that the old man is dead, and then live out the resurrected life.

In Romans 5:17, we learn that this life is not obtained after we die but *now!*

> For if by the one man's offense death reigned through the one, much more will those who receive abundance of grace and of the gift of righteousness reign in life through the One, Jesus Christ.
>
> For if we have been united together in the likeness of His death, certainly we also shall be in the likeness of His resurrection…
>
> Romans 6:5a

If I have not been "united together" with Christ in His death, then I am not saved! In Christ, I died. Christ died as me—not simply for me—so that I can have His life. Christ took upon himself what I had coming to me, so that I could receive what He had coming to Him. If I died in Christ, then I live in Christ and this life will not be my own life (of my own nature or of my own strength) but Christ living through me. The mark of Christ in our lives is a resurrected, powerful, righteous life- not the suffering of a cross!

This amazing kingdom life will first be a life of love—a love life. Love is the reason God sent Jesus, who is life. "For God so *loved* the world that He sent…" This abundant life will be a life filled with the fruit of the Spirit. I once had a professor who put it this way: Joy is love dancing; peace is love resting; patience is love understanding; kindness, goodness and gentleness are love in action; faithfulness is love in battle; meekness and self-control are love reigning in my life. Would you say you experience this?

Many Christians still hold to the belief that we are to be forgiven of our sins and then suffer or hang on until the Lord returns or we die. This thought of Christian living undermines what Jesus taught on the abundant life. Jesus was not teaching that everything, all the time, was going to be easy, but that in all things we should experience the life of Christ. Revival or renewal is simply the people of God awakening to the life of Christ in them. What does renewal look like to your life? Christ! Christ continually manifesting Himself to you and through you is biblical revival and kingdom living.

Life and Truth

I want to look at how truth and life are related. Jesus said that His words were spirit and life (John 6:63b). Every word Jesus spoke was spirit in nature and was pregnant with life. Jesus, who is the Word of God made flesh, said that He is the way, the *truth*, and the *life* (John 14:6a). These verses teach us a simple truth. Truth brings life. Jesus's words were truth and they contained life.

One of the largest schools of thought in our society is that all truth is relative. This thought implies that what is true for me does not have to be true for you. It says, "I don't need to push my "truths" on others but allow others to believe whatever is "truth" to them." One can believe in God and another can deny His existence and both are true. This means there are no absolutes. This means I can live as I want. No God, no moral absolutes, I'm free—so I think. However, this belief has one great problem—the principle of no absolutes is an absolute! I am not a philosopher, but if a theory contradicts itself in its primary principle, then it must not be valid.

Philosophies like these leave people feeling smart but also dead. When a person tries to adjust truth to validate a lifestyle or soften the guilt of his conscience, he makes a grave mistake. In doing this, He may ease his conscience momentarily but he will lock himself into a spiritual, emotional, and relational death. Truth is the vehicle of life; therefore, adjusting our lives to the truth (Jesus's Words) will bring real, abundant life.

If you go into the operating room to have your tonsils removed and the doctor begins to draw his incision marks on your chest, there might be some questioning. You might say, "What are you doing, Doc? My tonsils are up here!" to which the doctor replies, "What does it matter? For you they are up there, for me they are down here!" Would you stay for the surgery? No, because based on the truth that your tonsils are not located in your chest, you believe the doctor does not know what he is doing. You base your evaluation of the Doctor on truth.

Truth, in the way that the Bible defines it, is not simply the absence of lies but is used to mean "ultimate reality." Truth, as it will be used in the remainder of this book, will be God's Word. Not simply the Scriptures, as we will discover, but the concept, idea, or deepest reality that is being communicated through His Word. Therefore, truth is central to the gospel and to having abundant life. If truth is central to life, then it is central to revival and renewal.

Early in Part One, I mentioned that when the church clings to what God has said at the expense of what He is saying, she sacrifices her young on the altar of traditions. This is the reason why: truth brings life. Bill Johnson says that faith comes by hearing, not by having heard. To reinforce this thought, Jesus said, "Man shall not live by bread alone but by every word that proceeds out of the mouth of God" (Matthew 4:4). Notice the present tense. When the church stops listening and obeying what God is saying in the present, life ends and death begins. The fresh Word of God is life to us.

I am not saying that the Bible is what God was saying and now He is saying something different. What I am saying is the freshness of the Bible comes when the Holy Spirit breathes on the Scriptures. Furthermore, God speaks outside of the Scriptures, just never contradicting to them. He may contradict your or my interpretation of the Scriptures but never the Scriptures themselves.

Pursuing Truth

The pursuit of truth is the pursuit of a person—and not just any person, but Jesus. The great news about truth is that He came looking for us! Jesus loves us! Truth loves us! Truth knows our name, knows everything about us. If I am in Christ, then I am in truth. If Christ is in me (Colossians 1:27), then truth is in me! What then is our pursuit? The pursuit is for revelation.

Revelation is the "unveiling" or "disclosing" of truth. Truth cannot be learned or earned. It does not come by intellectual exercise and is not discovered, but revealed or given. Second Timothy 3:7 says of certain men that they are "always learning and never coming to the knowledge of truth." A person can be constantly growing, mentally learning, and never come to truth.

We must take what is true and make it our core values. This is adjusting our value system to God's, creating an atmosphere for Him to work in and through us. We must pursue revelation and remember-revelation only comes by the Spirit of God (1 Corinthians 2:10a).

Revelation

> That the God of our Lord Jesus Christ, the Father of glory, may give to you the spirit of wisdom and revelation in the knowledge of Him, the eyes of heart being enlightened, that you may know…
>
> Ephesians 1:17

Paul does not pray for a fresh move of God or a fresh outpouring, even though those things would have been great. He prayed that the saints of Ephesus would experience the spirit of wisdom and revelation. Revelation would enlighten their hearts. Revelation knowledge relates to the heart, not to the mind. The heart being enlightened is what will make the Ephesians know. This word *know* in the Greek refers to a experiential knowledge. Revelation enlightens the heart (core) so the Ephesians could experience God. I spend more time looking at Paul's prayer to the Ephesians in appendix A.

One of the most deadly viruses in the church is mental assent, which is seen when someone says they believe the Word of God but rarely make adjustments in their lives to act on the Word. This person mentally gives their allegiance to the Scripture and to God but lives as a practical atheist—the Word of God is not "lifed out" in their daily life. When one first hears or reads God's Word, it is information competing against information. However, God intends for it to be more. Let's look at three Greek words used to describe God's Word.

The first is *logos*. Logos can have many meanings, from the written word to instruction or speech, but the basic fundamental meaning is "the expression of thought, concept, or idea" (Vine's 683). Whether the word is spoken or written does not matter, both uses of the word are in the New Testament. What it does mean is the basic concept or thought being communicated. Take for example a family returning from a visit to Frontier City, a family theme park in Oklahoma City. I ask them, "Did you have fun?" to which the mother responds, "We had a great time." The idea is yes, they did, but the children respond to my question differently. They say, "Wow!" with their hands high in the air. The idea or concept expressed is still yes, they had a good time, but they used different words, even other means (using body language), but the concept or idea is still communicated as "Yes."

Another word used in the New Testament for God's Word is *rhema*. Rhema denotes "that which is spoken; what is uttered in speech" (Vine's). It is my conviction that this usage for "word" can be referring to the revelation knowledge that comes by the Spirit of God. In Ephesians 6:17 Paul encourages believers to take up the "sword of the Spirit, which is the word (*rhema*) of God." Notice the sword of the Spirit and *rhema* of God.

There is a third word that is used for "scripture." The word is *graphé*. Graphé means to write. Jesus used this word in John 5:39, "You search the Scriptures (*graphé*), for in them you think you have eternal life…" It is also used in Romans 4:3, "For what does the Scripture (*graphé*) say? "'Abraham believed God, and it was accounted to him for righteousness.'" This word is almost always used to describe God's written record.

You may be wondering where this is going. The scriptures (graphé) plus revelation (rhema) equals truth (logos). Jesus said, If you abide (remain, live, dwell) in My Word (logos) you are my disciple indeed. And you shall know the truth, and the truth shall make you free (John 8:31–32). When the Word of God is breathed on by the Spirit of God, the result is truth. When truth is received by faith it produces abundant life.

Intimacy and Revelation

Revelation is an invitation to encounter the Revealer (John 5). I explained this in Part One. However, the fruit of the encounter is to be intimacy with the God the Holy Spirit. To really know my wife, I experience her. If all I ever knew was facts about her, there would be no life to the relationship. "No longer do I call you servants, for a servant does not know what his master is doing; but I have called you friends, for all things that I heard from My Father I have make known (revealed) to you" (John 15:15). This statement teaches that revelation flows from intimacy. Friend to friend relationships are more intimate than slave to master relationships. As they grew intimate with Jesus, they had revelation. Revelation is both an invitation into intimacy, and in that intimacy, more revelation comes.

The Bible is a closed book without the Holy Spirit. We must have revelation (which only comes by the Holy Spirit) to receive from the Bible. The logos of God comes with the power to perform. We need the Word and we need relationship with, and revelation of, the Holy

Spirit in order to know truth! Jesus said, "However, when He, the Spirit of truth, has come, He will guide you into all truth…" (John 16:13). One of the Holy Spirit's roles is to guide the believer into truth. We should trust the Spirits ability to lead us into truth more then our ability to follow. Truth then is never arrived at or revealed to the believer without the Holy Spirit. This Word and Spirit combination brings truth, and when truth is properly responded to, it is demonstrated through power, which results in life!

To help a person practically start, start with the Word (information). Next, meditate on the Word. Eastern meditation is emptying your mind, while biblical meditation is filling your mind with the Word of God. Many Christians think they do not know how to meditate, but if you know how to worry you know how to meditate. Worry is meditation on the inferior reality. This biblical meditation is what Solomon meant in Proverbs 4:20–23, "My son, give attention to my words… keep them in the midst of your heart… for they are life to those who find them… for out of it (your heart) spring the issues of life.

The Holy Spirit unveiling and revealing truth to us is the only way truth comes. When truth is accompanied by faith, it produces transformation in us. Receiving revelation is not the end! Revelation handled incorrectly leads to religion.

The Danger of Religion

Do you remember the parable of the sower and the seed? In Matthew 13:18–23, Jesus explains this parable. "When anyone hears the word (logos, truth) of the kingdom, and does not understand it, then the wicked one comes and snatches away what was sown (which was truth) in his heart" (v. 19). If a person hears the truth and does not "understand" it the devil can steal it away! Notice that the devil steals it out of the person's heart and not their head!

Biblical understanding is different than intellectual understanding. For example, the Bible says, "By faith we understand that the worlds were framed by the Word of God, so that the things which are seen were not made of things which are visible" (Hebrews 11:3). I do not understand with my mind how something was created out of nothing, but by faith it makes since!

The word *understand,* in Matthew 13:19, is the word *suniemi.* It means to set or bring together, as in a hostile or combatant sense, to put the perception with the thing perceived (Strong's). Looking at the origin of the word might be more helpful. *Suniemi* is made up of two words; sun which is "with" or "union" and *heimi* which means "to send or to go," meaning union with sending; to set something together for the purpose of going or acting. This word can imply two meanings, both of which I believe are helpful. The first is to set. We must take the Word sown and set it in our hearts. Keep it there, meditate on it, or chew on it. Remember, "As a man thinks in his heart so is he" (Proverbs 23:7).

The second meaning is to connect the Word sown together with a person's life. This might better be referred to as application. Say I was to teach on the Father's love and a person hearing this teaching comes to the revelation that they need to receive this love and give this love. However, they leave the service, and make no adjustments to their life to focus on receiving this love, and no adjustments to their relationships to give this love. Then a month later, they hear a sermon on the Father's love from another teacher, and they might say, "Well, this teaching is for someone else. I've had this revelation." However, they are deceived. The devil will have snatched it from their heart and left it in their head so that they think they "understand" it. Hearing without doing locks people into form without power, which is religion!

The renewed mind proves the will of God. The person mentioned above thinks their mind is renewed, but it is not. This is how men are "always learning and never able to come to the knowledge of the truth" (2 Timothy 3:7). Jesus said, "You diligently study the scriptures because you think that by them you possess eternal life. These are the scriptures that testify about me, yet you refuse to come (action) to me to have life (John 5:39–40, NIV)." The people Jesus is talking to knew the Scripture (*graphē*); many of them had the first five books of the Bible memorized. But they would not come. They had mental assent or head knowledge, but never made the move to act, they never made it to faith in Jesus!

Becoming What We Tried to Avoid

I have heard it said, "reacting to an error breeds more error." We are to live responding to truth not reacting to everyone else's error. People who react to error have the potential of becoming what they were working to avoid; they can become deceived.

Take religion, for an example. A man grows up in a church that taught him that he had to act right in order for God to love him and accept him. Now this is an error of religion. If this statement were true, then we would be earning grace—which violates grace! So, one day this man is reading his Bible and praying and out of this time, questions begin to arise. Then those questions grow into concerns. Over time the Holy Spirit brings revelation of the truth and then the man becomes alive with the truth of grace through faith!

If this man is not careful, his experience will train his heart to question everything! "If I have been deceived once, it could happen again," he thinks to himself. So, he questions everything, even God. The mind is not to be our leader, but our servant, a great tool in the hands of the Master. However, this man makes his mind his master, instead of Jesus. He questions and has more questions than answers, which leads to doubting and ultimately doubting what God is saying. Over time, the man had impressions that were from God but would question himself out of obeying them. Because he does not want to be deceived he winds up doing nothing, which is probably all the deceiver was out to do to this man anyway.

Now think about this with me: how did the church or pastor arrive at the conclusion that this man had to earn Gods love? They probably only taught what made sense in their head. They obviously did not come to that conclusion by the revelation of the Holy Spirit. They were led by their intellect and not by the Holy Spirit. It made sense to them. What did not make sense was how grace and unconditional love worked together with holiness and sanctification. In their reasoning, God loves us based on our action. Instead of spending more time praying and seeking, they spent it preaching and teaching. They wind up teaching error, not intentionally, and the damage is done.

This man has become the very thing he was trying to avoid. He has become like the group he was trying not to be. Different beliefs but the same fundamental problem: trusting their intellect over trusting God. He reacted to an error and made another error. His error had its starting point in the fact that he thought he arrived at truth by his questions, by his logic. However, the questions were birthed because he began to hang out with a person: Jesus. He started reading, praying, and enjoying his relationship with Jesus and out of that relationship the questions arose.

If a person does not want to fall for a counterfeit dollar, then they must study the real bill well. If you do not want to be deceived then cling to truth. We must never give our questions more authority or influence in our lives than the revelation of Jesus we have had. We should ask Jesus about what we don't understand and then wait. Wait by enjoying grace, loving on Jesus, and in due season, He will reveal to you the answer. Do *not* try to answer a question that God is not answering! Wait, I say; wait on the Lord!

Power

The kingdom of God is not in word, but in power.

1 Corinthians 4:20

Jesus states in Matthew 28:18 that "all authority" has been given to Him. If He has all authority, then the devil has none! Zero. The only time the devil has power over a person is when they believe his lies. The devil is both a liar and the father of lies. His only hope is to deceive people into believing him. If all the devil's power is in the lie, then all the power we need to conquer the enemy is truth.

The devil has already been defeated. Jesus won! But he still roams the earth; he is defeated, but has not yet been arrested. Our job on this planet is to co-labor with the conquering King, enforcing the victory of the cross. I am not fighting for victory but from the position of victory that Christ has already won. I am not fighting to be healed—I am the healed victor that the devil wants to make sick. I am not working to become righteous—I am the righteousness of Christ that the devil wants to render powerless by trying to make me work for what I already have!

Power is the ability to manifest truth! "…As His divine power has given to us all things that pertain to life and godliness…" (2 Peter 1:3). If truth brings life and "His divine power" gives us all we need for life, then power is manifesting truth. "If you abide in My word (truth), you are My disciples indeed. And you shall know the truth, and the truth shall make you free" (John 8:31–32). This freedom is a result of power; manifested truth. The kingdom is in power not word. Why? Because power is the manifestation of the Word!

Jesus walked in truth and therefore walked in power. I hope the importance of this does not escape your notice because it means that we must pursue truth and the manifesting of that truth in our lives to walk in power. Pursuing power over truth is like having the President fly to your house and when he arrives, you focus on Air Force One (the airplane). You would miss out on the point—the President is here, at your house! Power is the means by which truth is manifested, which results in life, and if I am focused on the means (power), it could hinder me from appropriating the substance (life, which is renewal).

Every demonstration of power is a display of truth. Every time someone is healed, delivered, or has an encounter with God, truth is being manifested. I encourage you in this: any time you experience power, be sure to ask for the truth that is being communicated! God gives signs and wonders. Signs point to a greater reality, which is truth, and wonders make us wonder what truth is being communicated.

FAITH

All Things Are Possible?

Do you ever have trouble believing the bible? I must confess that I can read the bible, declare that it is true, but not really believe the implications of what it is teaching. The Bible says that with God all things are possible (Matthew 9:26). I have no trouble believing that, He is like ... God. But Jesus says that all things are possible to him who believes (Mark 9:23). Both statements point out all things are possible. I can believe that all things are possible for God, but can I equally believe that all things are possible to him that believes? Jesus did! Practically, this means that through faith the things that are possible to God are made equally possible to the one who believes, though never separate from God.

I have always tried hard to be a Bible-believing Christian, but Jesus is not making that easy. To be biblically accurate we must accept that through faith, what is possible for God becomes possible for the believing one. Therefore, studying faith would be worth our time and effort.

Blinded By Sight

The Bible says that faith is the evidence of things not seen (Hebrews 11:1). Faith relates to the invisible realm just as our five senses connect us to the visible realm. The Scriptures use faith solely and exclusively to relate to two realities: God Himself and His Word. "For we walk by faith, not by sight" (2 Corinthians 5:7). Faith and sight are mutually exclusive. If we are walking by faith then we do not need sight, if we have sight we do not need faith. The world says seeing is believing, but the Bible teaches differently.

David said, "I would have lost heart, unless I believed that I would see the goodness of the Lord in the land of the living" (Psalm 27:13). Which one came first, seeing or believing? Jesus taught the same thing, "Did I not say to you that if you would believe you would see the glory of God?" (John 11:40). Faith preceeds seeing. Faith enables us to see the invisible and inadvertently enables us to endure when the visible world offers us no hope or encouragement. "While we do not look at the things which are seen, but at the things which are not seen. For the things which are seen are temporary, but the things which are not see are eternal" (2 Corinthians 4:18). We are not to look at the visible but to look at the invisible. Faith gives us the ability to see things that cannot be seen in the natural. If we walk by what is seen in the natural or by our natural eyes, we will be blinded to what God is doing in the invisible. Therefore, Christians can be blinded by their natural sight.

Furthermore, this verse teaches us that what is seen in the natural is temporary while what is not seen is eternal. Remember our definition of idolatry: valuing the temporary above the eternal. When we operate out of our natural senses while God's Word is saying the opposite, we have committed idolatry. When I walk by my senses and not solely by God's Word, I have chosen unbelief, which is faith in the inferior realm and is sure to fulfill itself.

Faith: A Christian's Home

Paul devotes an entire epistle to argue half of one verse, in one of the smallest books in the Old Testament. The verse: "The just shall live by faith" (Hab. 2:4). This verse was worth all the effort and time that the old apostle gave it, for in it is a truth that will revolutionize the way mankind will live. This simple verse reveals that those who stand before God just or righteous are not there because of their obedience to the law, but by their faith in Christ Jesus.

Righteousness is a gift (Romans 5:17). It is not earned by works nor achieved by keeping the law without transgression. Righteousness is available apart from the law in Christ, to be received by faith. This is what it means for the just to live by faith. They live everyday with the awareness they are righteous before God, apart from their performance because Jesus has died for their sin, and by faith they declare Christ is our only hope of righteousness.

To live by faith is to make faith in Christ your home, dwelling in the reality that I please God in Christ. This one truth awakens us to new reality: by faith in Christ, I have become the righteousness of Christ (2 Corinthians 5:21), and now apart from my works, I stand before God with the same standing as Christ, for I am His righteousness. Wow, what a great God.

To develop a kingdom culture, we must have a deep understanding of how we stand in front of the King! Faith is always in the heart not in the head, for with the heart one believes unto righteousness (Romans 10:10). When this truth-that we are righteous before God by faith alone-seeps down past our intellect and into our hearts, becoming a core value, we will cultivate a culture that will walk like Jesus!

Faith in Action

Faith without works is dead. This does not mean that we are to go find some works and do them. This means that believing a truth in the heart will always bring about a certain action. I want to briefly give you an insight into appropriating God's promises. Everything we could possibly need to live in and live out (advance) the kingdom, God has given to us in the form of promises. So, here are some steps that have helped me.

First, ask the Holy Spirit to direct you to a particular promise that applies to your situation and meets your needs. This will often take some time of praying and searching the Scriptures. Secondly, when the promise is revealed, obediently fulfill any conditions attached to the promise. In Romans 8:28, for example, God promises to work all things out for good, but only for those who love Him and are called according to His purpose. His purpose is revealed in the next verse, " ... to be conformed into the image of His Son." If you do not love God and are not yielding yourself to Him to be conformed into Jesus, then God is not obligated to work all things out for your good.

Last, after you find the promise and fulfill the conditions, trust. Trust by saying that whatever God has promised you is yours regardless if you see it, taste it, touch it, or feel it. God cannot lie. So find, fulfill, and trust by confessing what God says is true. All truth must be responded to by faith. Faith simply brings what is real into our experience.

Mixing Faith

For indeed the gospel was preached to us as well as to them; but the word (truth) which they heard did not profit them, not being mixed with faith in those who heard it.

Hebrews 4:2

Faith has fallen on hard times. It has been worked over and looked over, both ignored and idolized. Faith is important but never more important than truth. Jesus said in Matthew 4:4, "Man shall not live by bread alone, but by every word (truth) that proceeds from the mouth of God." However, Paul writes that the just shall live by faith (Romans 1:17). By which one then do I live—faith or truth? The answer is ... yes. I have faith in every word (truth) that proceeds out of His mouth. I cannot believe God for a corvette if He has not promised one to me. Faith begins and ends where the Word of God (truth) is known. The Spirit of God must come and pull back the veil (revelation) and show us the great and numerous things Christ has accomplished through His life, His cross, His death, His resurrection, and His seating, because we would not believe it any other way.

Many believers think they have a faith problem. However, it could be a truth problem. Imagine I had this ladder that rested against the top of a fifty-foot wall. I started up the ladder without any reservation, but when I reached the halfway point in my climb the ladder broke and I descended into injury. Did the ladder break for my lack of faith? No, I had enough faith in it to risk my life. I did not have a faith problem but a truth problem. The object of my faith (the ladder) was not worthy of the faith I gave it. If I had known the truth of the ladder, I would not have started the climb and have fallen.

Notice that Paul in his prayer for the saints did not pray for more faith. He asks for "wisdom and revelation in the *knowledge* of Him." 2 Peter 1:3 says, "... His divine power has given to us *all things* that pertain to life and godliness, *through* the *knowledge* of Him ..." Furthermore, in verse 5 it says, "... add to your faith virtue, to virtue *knowledge* ..." Hosea 4:6: "My people are destroyed for lack of knowledge ..." Proverbs 29:18 states, "Where there is no revelation (truth), the people cast off restraint ..." Jesus reported that faith as a mustard seed can move mountains. Could He be trying to say that size is not the issue? The smallest seed of faith moves mountains. The need is for revelation knowledge of what our faith was created, or called by God, to do.

A friend of mine once shared with me an analogy that C. H.

Spurgeon used to illustrate faith, which I have adopted. Picture a son standing on the edge of a swimming pool. The boy's father is in the pool with his hands raised towards the boy and requests the boy to jump. The boy hears "jump." It registers at a cognitive level. The boy can think to himself, "My father told me to jump," but does the boy have faith? No. The boy can even mentally assent to the character of his father. He could reason, "My father never lies, he has never failed me. I can trust my father, who said 'Jump.'" Does he then have faith? No—not until there is the plunge from the side of the pool into the Father's arms has the boy illustrated faith!

Faith is the fruit of surrender, not effort. Faith comes by the Word of God (Romans 10:17). As we surrender our souls (mind, will, and emotions) to the Word of God, faith arises. Earlier I broke down the word *understanding*. The meaning of the word was to set or bring together for the purpose of going or acting. I believe faith is the simple connection of truth with obedience. This connection is like taking one end of an extension cord and connecting it to the power source. When truth, the source of power, connects with my obedience, the result is life. Faith is the connecting point! Faith is judging the character and Word of God correctly, which will lead to an action!

FREEDOM

Freedom is central to the kingdom of God. So much so, that Paul says that it is one of the driving reasons that Christ died. God did not die to control us but to set us free. Freedom has to do with choices and the ability to make them. God gave Adam and Eve choices in the garden. He did not put the tree of knowledge of good and evil on top of a mountain, or in the dessert, He placed it right in the middle of the garden. God does not guard us from temptation; He makes a way out of it (1 Corinthians 10:13), creating a choice. God does not do this because He wants to see us fail, but because He wants to reward us for making the right decision.

Freedom has to do with the right to make our own choices. Independence has to do with rulership. God has made us free so we can choose to be dependent on Him. I have stated earlier that the great sin of man is independence—the self-righteous audacity to think we can successfully rule ourselves. Man left alone will always produce his own prison. Freedom cannot be successfully defined outside of God. Man, acting completely independent of God will eventually be in bondage.

Man is not qualified to judge for himself, because he lacks fore-knowledge or complete understanding. He does not know whether a decision will lead to bondage or not. Take cigarettes for example. Back in the early days many smoked, not knowing the damage it would cause. Man functioned freely and independently and because of his incompetency to know the ultimate end of something, his choices land him in addiction. To really be free, one must choose to surrender. Therefore, true freedom is a direct result of true surrender to King Jesus!

I had a student one time come to me and begin to tell me that he did not need God and all His rules. I began to ask him what rules he was referring too. He said, "Like 'em ten commandments." I responded, "Thou shall not murder … Yeah, that's a bummer, huh?" He did not seem to be impressed with my theological slang. So, I asked him if he had both parents at home. He informed me that his dad had cheated on his mom and she recently kicked him out. I asked him, "Did your dad committing adultery on your mother make your life more fulfilling?" He said, "No, it actually has messed things up." I responded, "I bet. God does not give us rules to confine us, but so that we can ultimately be satisfied. He tells us not to commit adultery because he knows that it will inevitably crush and hurt people."

You see, God is really good and really smart. He knows that the ultimate satisfaction of man will only come as they are in relationship with Him. Secondly, He knows the things to avoid because of the pain and hurt they bring upon people. Imagine if everyone in the world would obey God for one day. No one would be hurt, no divorce, no affairs, no break-ins or murders, nothing stolen, not a person drunk, not even a hurtful word would be spoken. In fact, heaven would visit earth. This is freedom. If everyone would obey God, everyone would be free to live and live it would be!

The real need behind advancing the kingdom is teaching saints how to steward their freedom well. We need to make the decisions that line up with heaven's value system, knowing that, despite what we may see, lining up our value system with heaven's will be the best thing for us! The kingdom has its own values that oppose many of the world's values. If we can teach and model for people how to adjust their value systems to heaven's, they will begin to reap the benefits of heaven and live in the highest and most satisfying abundant life.

The Beauty of Grace

Instead of placing strict rules on people and trying to manipulate their behavior from the outside (law or guard), the attitude of grace is to come along side (guide) someone and empower them. Religion demands, while grace draws. Religion restricts in order to get people to conform, while grace empowers in order to see people transformed! Only one expresses God's deep value for freedom. To be a people of grace, we must allow people to make mistakes, while we go after connecting their hearts to God.

A tired, defeated, worked-over young lady comes down the aisle to receive Christ. She has on too much makeup, her pants look like they were painted on, her shirt should not be worn in public, and you can tell life has yanked her through a knothole. She has heard that Jesus can make sense of all of this and heal her broken heart. She yields her heart and life to Christ. Many would tell her, "Well, now you need to change your pants and shirt, remove some makeup, and start smiling because you're going to heaven." However, if she is forced to change her clothes and makeup (conformity) she will not have the heart connection needed to sustain the change. But if the people of God would come along side of her, love on her, regardless of her clothes, hair, and makeup and point her to Jesus, He will eventually change her. If we can simply connect her heart with Papa God, He will change her from the inside out, and there will be nothing the world, the flesh, or the devil can do, because she has been transformed by grace. If she is restricted by religion to conform, it will not last, but when she is empowered by grace, the transformation will be eternal!

Grace has this beautiful way of tearing down the strongest walls without using one tool. Grace can make the strongest of armies surrender without using a weapon. The liberals think grace is God's willingness to look past our problems. The religious group believes grace is for salvation, and dealing with our problems is simply left up to us! But biblical grace is God's ability and willingness to come along side of us and tear down our problems Himself. There is no defense to selfless love. May God cultivate in us a deep value and confidence in His wonderful grace to transform.

The Choices We Make

I call heaven and earth as witnesses today against you, that I have set before you life and death, blessing and cursing; therefore chose life, that you and your descendants may live; that you may love the Lord your God, that you may obey His voice, and that you may cling to Him, for He is your life…

Deuteronomy 30:19–20

Because God values freedom He gives us choices. Because He values it, we ought to also, and take the choices laid before us seriously. When God speaks, He takes it seriously and so should we. In this verse, God calls heaven and earth to witness what He is saying. We should tremble at the thought of this glorious God King speaking to us. "Hear the word of the Lord, you who tremble at His word" (Isaiah 66:5). As a matter of fact, this verse implies that those who tremble at His Word hear God's voice more than those who do not. It does not say, "Tremble all who hear," but hear the Word of the Lord, those who tremble! God is not stingy with His voice, but He is a good steward of it. He will not speak to people who won't heed His words. Many people are not hearing God (present tense) because they did not obey what they have heard! As Henry Blackaby has so eloquently put, "If you are not hearing from God go back to the last thing He said."

God made it very clear to the Israelites what choice should be made. Here in this passage, God makes obedience an issue of choice. Every time God speaks, we are presented with the very same choices as the Israelites. Every time you study your Bible, hear a sermon that is from God, or receive a revelation from God, a choice of life and death must be made. As you read this now, I believe that a choice must be made.

Will you choose life or death? Blessing or cursing? It is not a matter of His love towards you. His love is not based on conditions. He loves you whether you choose life or death; however, He really wants to see you walking in the quality of life He died for you to have!

God has made us free. No one can control us. God does not want to and the devil cannot without our agreement. If someone sticks a gun in your mouth and tells you to deny Christ you still have two choices! No one can control you without you giving them that control.

Blame is simply the admission to where we surrendered our control. When we blame someone we are saying, "We cannot change unless they do." We are showing who we have given our freedom too. You may have heard the expression, "You are pushing my buttons." You only push buttons on things you are controlling. We must have the core value that we are free. There is nothing anyone can do that can move us out of honor, love, and peace. "You're making me angry!" is a lie; we choose to be angry. You and I are free to make these choices. This is maturity: to learn how to steward the amazing freedom God has died to give us!

Many may not like this because it puts a lot of responsibility on us. We choose what our hearts meditate on. We choose to abide in His Word or not. Remember, the devil is a liar and he will try to convince you that you are not free to choose. This is a lie. The devil may try to convince you that it is all God's responsibility to change your heart. God will change your heart as you choose to meditate on His Word. Your response determines the effectiveness of His Word in your life. Any theology that places all responsibility on God, removing all our responsibility towards Him, is not the theology of the Bible!

HONOR

"Honor all people."

1 Peter 2:17

There are two means of government: control or honor. These two means can also apply to relationship. A person functions in a relationship by one of these two: controlling or honoring. A controlling person is normally afraid that if he/she is not in control then he/she will either be hurt or be left with their needs unmet. A person who honors others allows them the freedom to make decisions while placing importance on them. When we give honor, apart from performance, we are not thinking about our needs but meeting the other person's needs. The only consistent way to motivate a person is to meet their deepest need. When another person's needs are met, they will be motivated to meet others' needs. Giving honor, even when people do not deserve it, sounds crazy to a nation that has been taken advantage of. However, there are two simple reasons to give this type of honor: every person is created in the image of God, and we give honor because we are a people of honor.

Everyone is created in the image of our God and that has to have some sort of lasting effect. We must honor people simply for this fact: they are an expression of the creativity and love of our

God. Every person walking on planet earth is loved and desired by God. In fact, He loves every single person so much that He has already paid for their sin (John 3:16, 1 John 2:2). Not only are they loved by God, but they are created by Him and for Him. If a friend of mine deeply loves and admires a certain person and I meet this person without my friend being present, I find it my normal response to honor the person based on my friend's love and admiration. Now, as friends of God should we not do the same. We shall give honor to all people simply because our Friend loves and admires His creation.

Next, we honor people apart from performance, because we are a people of honor. A *people of love* love loveless people. A *people of honor* honor those who appear undeserving because it is who they are. Just as God loves us into loving Him when we are unloving, we honor the un-honorable into being honorable. When God loves us when we are unlovely, He calls us to our destiny, to be a person who is in love with God. When we honor a person who does not deserve it we call them into their destiny, a person of royalty.

All saints have this unique privilege to be adopted as sons. (Bear with me ladies, you work on being a son and I will work on being a bride.) As sons, the Bible says we are heirs with Christ (Galatians 4:7). This means we are royalty, a people who are princes and princesses. Every person in the kingdom of God is an heir. This being the case, honor should be a natural expression of the kingdom. We are a people of honor and we will give honor as an overflow of who we are.

Honoring, Not Flattering

As a people of honor we must learn to honor without flattering. Honoring a person has nothing to do with exaggeration, manipulation, or control. In fact, it is the direct opposite. To properly honor a person is to see a person through God's eyes. We find out what is honorable about a person and honor it. Never is it honoring to make something up or say empty words to flatter. We pray and ask God how He sees a person and begin to say what He is saying in order to encourage and build that person up. Let the world, the flesh, and the devil kick their teeth in, discourage them, lie, and dishonor them. Let the church be a place of honor and encouragement.

I actually believe that a culture of honor will produce dreamers! When people actually believe they can accomplish their dreams, we have begun to empower. A culture of honor allows dreams to be birthed and shared without being attacked, whereas the dreamless will be a people of discouragement and dishonor. There is nothing like the wrath of the dreamless.

Honor Brings Life

There is another interesting principle about honor: it brings life. The Bible teaches us to honor our father and mother and we will have a long life. I believe the principle is: honor brings life. If you have a broken relationship and desire to see that relationship restored; start honoring the person. As you sincerely honor that person it brings life to that relationship. Remember, this is not manipulation. If I only honor a person to generate a certain response, I am manipulating. I honor because there is an honorable quality or because I am a person of honor, never to control.

However, it is good to know that when the dynamic of honor is introduced into a relationship it will bring life to that relationship. When honor is absent, other dynamics have to be introduced. Many relationships lack honor, and when honor is not present in a relationship, control is the only other alternative. Some move into control because they feel if they do not, then their needs will go unmet. If control is the means, then manipulation will be present and often violence will be introduced. This is where the philosophy "whoever has the biggest gun calls the shots" comes from. This has been the nature of man since the fall. Whoever has the power of violence will have control; but Jesus came with a new paradigm: Love. Love honors. Isn't that ironic? Man has operated with the manipulation theory for years, but God who has the power to destroy us with a word, does not use that power to manipulate our behavior. Instead, He, who has the biggest sword, willfully submitted Himself to the cross. In doing so, He proved how valuable we are to Him. Silver or gold could not purchase us; it took His life and He was willing to pay the price.

The cross proves we are valuable apart from our performance. The cross shows my performance deserved death, but I am valuable enough to Him for Him to die to ransom me. Therefore, I am valuable to God, apart from my performance. What a wonderful God! May we learn to be love and honor people the way God does.

Receiving Honor

One of the most humbling experiences in my life has been having my feet washed by another person. Some time ago, our church was restoring broken relationships with others. One relationship that had suffered was with a former youth pastor. Our church wrote a letter of repentance and invited him and his family to a service in their honor. Our entire church took turns washing this man's and his family's feet. It was a beautiful night of forgiveness and restoration. After we had honored him, he wanted to repent for some of the things he had done and honor our church. Instead of washing everyone's feet, he washed my feet as I represented the whole body. It is difficult sometimes to receive honor.

We must learn to receive honor properly. If you do not like receiving honor, you may not like heaven, because in heaven, you're going to be receiving a crown. Jesus both washed the disciples' feet and had His feet washed. We, like Jesus, have to be humble enough to give and receive. There is no room for this false humility that does not want any recognition at all! If I really want to be like Jesus, then

I have to want to be significant. Not famous or arrogant but impacting. Remember James taught, "Humble yourselves in the sight of the Lord, and He will lift you up" (James 4:10). If you don't want to be lifted up, then don't humble yourself. False humility will cheat you of your destiny by telling you that you are not worthy to be what He said you are. Pride will distract from you destiny by telling you to be something on your own, but true humility embraces destiny.

Humility is agreeing with God. When He says you have sinned, humility agrees. When He says we are more than conquerors and heirs of the King, humility agrees. Anything else is pride. Agreeing with God is walking with God, and walking with God is our greatest honor! May the Lord give you the grace to humble yourself and embrace the greatness to which He has called you!

When honor becomes one of the core values of the church, people will become what they were destined to be. We will begin to bring the best out of people instead of demanding conformity. Honor, as a core value, creates an environment that makes world-changers out of fishermen. May we all learn the way of honor.

DIVINE JUSTICE: OUR LOST CAUSE

Righteousness and justice are the foundations of Your throne...

Psalm 89:14

Justice is the foundation of our Father's throne. A throne is only fit for a king, so if it is the foundation of His throne, then it is the foundation to the kingdom. Isaiah 30:18 reads, "...For the Lord is a God of justice." Justice was also central to Jesus's ministry and purpose. Talking about Jesus, Isaiah stated, "A bruised reed He will not break, and smoking flax He will not quench; He will bring forth justice for truth. He will not fail nor be discouraged, till He has established justice in the earth..." (42:4–5). Jesus came to establish "justice for truth." He came to bring justice in the earth.

The psalmist speaks of the effects of injustice in Psalm 82. This psalm starts with God judging among the "gods." I believe the psalmist is using "Elohim" as judge. God is judging the judges. Why? "How long will you judge unjustly..." pretty much sums it up. God is judging the judges because they have judged unjustly. Verse 5 gives the effect of injustice, "all the foundations of the earth are unstable." All the earth is unstable because of injustice. Could it be the same today? What a significant impact justice has on the earth. If justice is this important to God, it ought to be important to us.

Restoration: Justice Made Practical

> The Spirit of the Lord God is upon me, because the Lord has anointed me to preach good tidings to the poor; He has sent me to bind up the brokenhearted, to proclaim liberty to the captives, and the opening of the prison to those who are bound; to proclaim the acceptable year of the Lord…
>
> Isaiah 61:1

Many may conclude the primary purpose of justice is punishment, however, that is not true. Justice is first to protect the righteous or the innocent. What then does justice look like when there is no one righteous? Jesus was the perfect model of divine justice, and He ultimately came to destroy the devil's work and reconcile sons and daughters to the Father (2 Corinthians 5:18,19).

About midmorning, on a hot Middle Eastern day, two guards come before the king, each restraining a hysterical woman. Each woman yelling at the other, with blatant disregard for the king, in whose presence they were. King Solomon, with patience, offers an opportunity for one woman to voice her injustice. She begins to tell the king how she awakened to find her son dead, but after further examination she realized that this was not her son but the son of the other woman who lived with her. As soon as the first woman finished her story the other woman voiced, "That's a lie. He was your son, this one is mine!" And then the first women fired back, "Liar, Liar." King Solomon had the ladies silenced and thought for a moment.

Many of us have been in a similar decision. Two kids fighting over something and all you have is a he-said-she-said problem. What to do? King Solomon came to a decision. The king said, "Cut the living baby in half, and give one half to this women and the other half to that woman." One of the woman yearned with compassion and said to the King, "Oh my Lord, give the living baby to the this woman, but please, please don't kill the boy." However, the other woman said, "Let the baby be neither mine nor yours, divide him!" King Solomon smiled and said, "Give the baby to the first lady, for it is her son." Then the Scriptures say, "All of Israel saw that the wisdom of God was in him (Solomon) to administer justice" (1 Kings 3:28).

What did justice do in this story? We have no account of the woman who stole the baby being punished. The Bible points out that justice restored the relationship. A son returns to his mother. I would like to suggest that this is the very heart of divine justice, restoration of relationship. In our time, God desires the blood of Jesus to touch our failures, mistakes, and offenses and those committed against us. When that happens restoration of relationship begins. This is how Jesus can "bind up the brokenhearted" and "set the prisoner free." Most people in prison deserve to be in prison. "Brokenhearted" could be speaking of someone who is innocently harmed and Jesus desires to bring divine justice to that situation. However, a prisoner is most likely guilty, but Jesus desires to see divine justice come to the prisoner too. How is freeing someone who is guilty, justice? When the blood of Jesus meets the offense or the sin the prisoner has committed, the blood cleanses him. So, someone did pay for the prisoner's crime: Jesus.

What does divine justice look like in a domestic violence situation? Let's say a husband is beating his wife. Divine justice appears when Jesus touches the wife and she learns deep biblical forgiveness and Jesus touches the husband's heart. The husband is probably hurting. Hurting people hurt people. When Jesus touches him and he is made whole and forgiven by the precious blood of Jesus, and the family can live together without fear or bondage, then divine justice has come, heaven has invaded earth, and the kingdom is demonstrated.

Martin Luther King Jr. had a picture of divine justice, "I have a dream that one day on the red hills of Georgia, the sons of former slaves and the sons of former slave owners will be able to sit down together at the table of brotherhood." "Together"-a picture of restored relationship, a picture of divine justice.

What does divine justice look like with abortion? It will not be a new law passed. Divine justice does not create more laws. However, if the only reason I do not kill my wife is because of a law, I still have marital problems! Divine justice appears when Jesus touches the woman who has had an abortion and she is forgiven and freed from the bondage of guilt. Then the next time she feels a baby move in her stomach she desires to have a relationship with her baby. When her desire for relationship with the baby inside of her is greater than her fear of not having the dad around, or the fear of not having enough money, then divine justice has come.

When the fatherless are restored to the father, when the tormented and the tormentor are forgiven and restored to right relationship, divine justice has occurred. When the blood of Jesus cleanses a Nazi of his guilt and shame, and then enables the Jew to forgive and they live together in right relationship, divine justice has come. When the lion lays with the lamb, heaven has invaded earth, the kingdom has come, and the God of peace has crushed Satan underneath our feet!

The Ministry of Reconciliation

Now all things are of God, who has reconciled us to Himself through Jesus Christ, and has given us the ministry of reconciliation, that is, that God was in Christ reconciling the world to Himself, not imputing their trespasses to them, and has committed to us the word of reconciliation.

2 Corinthians 5:18–19

As I stated in the opening paragraph of this section, I used to have a distorted view of God. I actually thought that Jesus died to save me from "Gawd." However, the above verse communicates another view of God. That God was actually in Christ reconciling us back to Himself. "Gawd" was not the bad guy. Love, grace, salvation, and reconciliation were actually His whole idea. If God had a body, I believe He would have scars on His hands too!

Divine justice is what Jesus came to do! To bring heaven to earth, destroy the devil's works, and bring many sons to the Father. He has committed to us this same ministry. "Committed" means He will not take it back. It is ours! So, how do we go about taking divine justice to the world?

God reconciled the world to Himself by "not counting men's sins against them." Now that we have this ministry should we use a different tactic than God? No way! If we are to reconcile the world to Jesus, it will be by "not counting their sins against them." Christians, who are to bring divine justice to the world, but will not enter into a situation because there is sin involved, have become burned out lights and flavorless salt. Sin in the Church is a little different but still requires grace and patience, but sin in the world is to be expected!

A young boy lay dead in an upper room. The boy's mother had sent for Elisha. When Elisha arrived He went in to where the boy was and began to pray. Then he lay on top of the boy eye to eye, mouth to mouth, hand to hand, and the flesh of the child became warm. Then he walked around the room praying some more and then repeated the act. This time the boy sneezed seven times and opened his eyes (2 Kings 4:32–36).

This story gives us a look at how ministry ought to be. No, not lying on little boys—that's more like a model for a lawsuit! This present generation in the church needs to learn the ministry of resurrection. Let's look at some truths that will equip us for a ministry of resurrection, both literally and figuratively.

The first and fundamental point is: Elisha was not intimidated by the death in the boy and was confident of the life in him. If the body of Christ is going to be cultivated into what Christ died to produce, we must have the revelation of His life in us. Many Christians are terrified of the expenditure another person represents. Everyone, I mean everyone, represents an expenditure to us. It can be intimidating and overwhelming for a person who does not have or know they have, a river flowing through them.

When a person tries to love or minister out of his own resource it will inevitably run out. But when a person simply receives the Father's love and then gives that love away, it never runs out. The Father wants to love through us, which means an endless supply! Burnout simply occurs when a person is giving more than they are receiving. Let's say a beggar walks up to you as you leave the grocery store. He asks, "Sir, do you have penny to spare?" You think to yourself, *What's a penny?* So, you give him a quarter and think to yourself, *Exceedingly, abundantly, above!* But what if the beggar had asked, "Sir, would you pay off the rest of my house? I just owe sixty thousand dollars, and you know I want spend it on booze. Please, I could really use the help." Well, now you are intimidated. Why? Because he is asking for a resource that you do not have available to give. At least I don't have sixty thousand dollars lying around to give, maybe you do. But the point is that we become intimidated when asked for something we do not possess to give.

The ministry of resurrection and reconciliation requires life. Many Christians are judging and condemning the world out of fear. They are intimidated by the expenditure the world represents. This fear masquerades as passion for holiness when really it lies in the absence of life. This fear is present when one does not have revelation and experience of an endless supply of life.

Our Father God wants to be our endless supply of life, love, and provision to continue the ministry of reconciliation. All He wants us to do is receive His love, life, and provision, and that will equip us to be the solution to the world's problems. The body of Christ must return to her confidence in the grace that brought her life. We must be more confident of the light in us than the darkness in the world. We are to be surer of the life in us then the death in the world and more impressed by the Christ in us then the devil in the world! We must have the core value that the life in us is more powerful than the death in the world.

Unbiblical judging is one of the schemes of the devil in hindering Christians in the application of divine justice. It is subtle and deadening. The devil wants us to make a final evaluation of a person. If you render something unchangeable you won't give of yourself to change it! If Satan can deceive a Christian into judging a person as unchangeable, then he has managed to deceive that Christian into agreeing with him. When we judge someone or something as unchangeable, we have agreed with the demonic influence behind it.

For example, suppose a man has a drinking problem. The demonic influences have lied to him. They have convinced this man that drinking is the only thing that helps the pain of the past hurts and mistakes. If I make a permanent judgment that this man is a drunk and will always be a drunk, then I will not give of myself to change him and then I have agreed with the demonic influence and the lies. Remember, the devil only has authority over a person when they believe his lies or agree with the lies. Lord, restore our confidence in your resurrected life in us!

The second point we draw from Elisha and the dead boy is that the Bible celebrates the body of the boy becoming warm rather than focusing on the fact the boy is still dead. Faith learns to focus on what God is doing, not what He isn't doing. The kingdom is easier to release in a atmosphere of thankfulness! Elisha was not offended that the boy did not jump up and dance but was encouraged that the boy became warm. Celebrate what God is doing and continue to pray for what He has yet to do. Jesus gave thanks for five loaves and two fish, and then there was a miracle. The unrenewed mind points out that two fish and some loaves does not feed a multitude, but the renewed mind thanks Him and witnesses a miracle. The renewed mind proves the will of God.

INCREASE AND PASSION

Representing Jesus

"As the Father has sent Me, I also send you."

John 20:21

Christianity is a revolution that counters the world's culture. It is not subcultural; it is countercultural. Subcultures are cultures that exist below (sub) or within the main culture. For example we have the main culture of the United States. A subculture is the Latino community. They exist within the framework of the main culture. The Latino community has different traditions, values, norms, even language, but they exist and function under the main culture. I grew up in southeastern Oklahoma. We had a people group with their own subculture: Rednecks. They have traditions, values, norms, and as Jeff Foxworthy has humorously pointed out, their own language, which is different than the main culture's.

The verse above carries with it great and exciting promises but is equaling sobering. Jesus had a very powerful impact on His culture. That is the good news. The bad news: they killed Him! Jesus countered His culture's traditions, like in Mark 7, when Jesus does not wash His hands to eat. Or when He heals on the Sabbath, knowing that it will make the Pharisees upset. We cannot forget the cosmic conflict-light verses darkness. Remember, Jesus won! However, He called us to be salt and light. Light by nature counters darkness. We are designed to counter the world's culture.

Persecution is a society's reaction to a challenge of its traditions or its culture. When someone or something threatens what is valuable or central to a culture it tends to cause a violent reaction. Often people will judge a nation unchangeable because that is easier than sacrificing to change it. If we are to accurately represent Jesus to this world around us we must not condemn the very people that the Father has sent us to reconcile to Him. It is at this point that some in the church begin to retreat and huddle away from the world. Why? If a group believes the world to be unchangeable than why counter the culture? Just retreat and huddle and wait for the rapture! I believe this is the problem with traditions in many churches. There is no reason to update your building, change services, or consider new methods. "Let's just protect our traditions and hang on till Jesus comes." A normal camper response!

God and Increase

The problem with protecting our traditions is that God is not interested in maintaining the status quo. God is not interested in protecting our culture or traditions. "Of the increase of His government and peace there will be no end…" (Isaiah 9:7). He is into increasing His kingdom by capturing the hearts of men, renewing the minds of men, and releasing these men. The church culture at large tends to value comfort. I know it does not seem that way with those wooden pews and all, but we do. However, God does not. He did not die to make us comfortable. God values increase. The parable in Luke 19 is a parable about the kingdom, and Jesus teaches on stewardship. Stewardship is not protecting what was given, but biblical stewardship is increasing what was given. The Master in the parable gave three servants minas. To one servant he gave ten minas, to another five, and to the last servant he gave one. When he returned, the one with ten increased his by ten. The one with five increased his five, but the one with one hid his and only had the one to give the Master. The Master calls the servant who hid his mina wicked (Luke 19:11–27). In this parable Jesus reveals God's heart for increase.

Furthermore, the point has been made that none of the armor of God mentioned in Ephesians 5 covers our back. God has designed us to move forward; increase. We were not designed to retreat or to huddle. A Christian is most vulnerable to the enemy when doing those two things. When we retreat the armor of God does not protect us. When we huddle together our backs are exposed to the enemy, not to mention that all the world sees is a bunch of rears. The proverb reads, "Where no oxen are, the trough is clean; but much increase comes by the strength of an ox" (Proverbs 14:4). We must value increase because God does, so we need oxen, which means there will be a mess. If I value clean stalls, then keep the oxen out, but there will be no increase for the King, and we saw how that worked out for the guy in Luke 19!

We must change our paradigm (way of thinking) from one of protecting to one of advancement (increase). The church must celebrate what God celebrates. He is looking and expecting for us to have increased what He has given us, not to have protected what He has given us.

Increase or Comfort

Retreating and huddling are common reactions of a culture that values comfort, a culture full of campers. Most people confuse being uncomfortable with not being at peace. However, go back and read the Scriptures again. When Jesus tells the disciples to have peace, or be of good cheer, or do not be afraid, they were always uncomfortable. God sent us the Comforter because He was planning on making us uncomfortable! Comfort is a relative term based on our traditions and culture. Peace is an internal reality based on His presence (Spirit) despite circumstances. This is why peace is a fruit of the Spirit. Uncomfortable is what I feel when something challenges my traditions, culture, or my values. I felt uncomfortable with the hole in the floor of the train in India. Peace comes from submission to and trust in God. Humility equips us with the wisdom to know the difference.

Fear appears to be commonplace in our present culture. Anxiety and worry, which is fear on Ritalin, plague many persons from the White House to the immigrant's house. They are a shot-glass amount of fear wanting to get you addicted enough to consume the whole bottle. Many Christians live in a constant state of fear, worry, and anxiety, so much so that it has become a normal part of our culture. The Bible says, "God did not give us a spirit of fear…" (2 Timothy 1:7). Fear is a spirit. If fear is a spirit and it did not come from God where else could it have come from? That is right; the kingdom of darkness.

Jesus said in Luke 12, "anxious minds." Worry and anxiety begin in the mind. Worry is simply meditation on the wrong things. The Bible offers an antidote; peace that passes understanding. Many Christians do not have peace because they are trying to understand. "If you want peace that passes understanding give God your right to understand," as I have heard said by Bill Johnson. Trusting God when I do not understand is to be normal for Christians. Think about this: how does the "peace that passes understanding" guard our minds, the thing we understand with? God gives us peace when we do not understand how He is going to show up. In doing so, His peace guards our mind from thinking that we have to understand to experience God! God's peace guards my mind from thinking it is the master. In the presence of this peace, I am focused on Him and not my understanding.

"I will be with you."—God

In order to be a part of this coming counter-cultural reformation we must bear all the fruit of the Spirit, but especially peace. Peace is a combat move that lands a huge blow to the enemy. Peace only comes as a result of hanging out with God. Valuing the presence of God (Holy Spirit) is the key to the kingdom, reformation, countering cultures, serving, loving, and creating a kingdom culture. If at the heart, we value His presence with us, we will have the peace, love, boldness, humility, and the power to transform the world. God brought national reformation through Gideon; one man who was dependent on the presence of God. When God wanted to rescue the Israelites from Egypt, He started by calling a stuttering shepherd to depend on Him, saying, "I will be with you."

We must create a church culture learned in how to impart passion for the person Holy Spirit. We are educated and experienced in imparting disciplines to people, but that is only half of the equation. There must be a combination of Word and Spirit, the mixture of which will create a firm foundation and a beautiful edifice of power, truth, creativity, encounters, and life! However, you cannot impart what do not have. If I only spent time with my wife because it was the "right thing to do," I'd have a marriage problem. Intimate relationships are to be lived out in passion. Discipline is needed when the passion may be gone for the day. But the disciplines are meant to hold us until the passion is rekindled. The evangelical community has become great at disciplines- and there is a valuable place for them- but that place is not in front of passion.

Getting Over What?

I remember I had the opportunity to lead a young man to the Lord. He did not grow up in church and I made the mistake of taking him to church where he did not know how to "act" properly. So, needless to say, I had people coming up to me saying things like this: "One day he'll get over it." *Get over it?!* You "get over" the hiccups or the runs, but not being ransomed, redeemed, delivered from the prison and translated into the kingdom; he became a child of God, transformed from a sinner into the righteousness of God, from dirty and alone to gloriously adopted and in relationship with Papa God! He should never "get over" that. That's our problem-we "got over it!"

Somewhere, somehow, someone has lied to us and convinced us that being passionate about God is not acceptable. Or at least it's not what the educated and the sophisticated people do. Well, as I have heard said, at that point our sophistication exceeds our intellect! If there is anything in the world to be passionate about it is the King and His kingdom. We must become child-like again, believe that our Dad can do anything; and actually be excited about the fact we get to hang out with Him.

Receiving and Imparting

Passion is our normal reaction to something we believe will satisfy our hearts. Passion is birthed when my needs are met. God is the answer to our needs. He is the satisfaction of our hearts. The Holy Spirit is here now, with the kingdom of God, ready to satisfy the hearts of men. To receive this kingdom that satisfies, is to simply yield to it, to allow it to overtake you. So, search it out in the Scriptures, meditate on it, and in due season the Holy Spirit will pull back the veil and you will see the glory of God in the kingdom of God.

When you see the kingdom of God, you will want to receive it. And you receive it by yielding to it, and yielding, by adjusting your value system to it. What is valuable to the kingdom must become valuable to us. We will always sacrifice for what is valuable to us. If quality of life is more valuable to us than the sanctity of life, then killing our elderly is closer than we think! If God becomes more valuable to us than anything else, we will sacrifice anything to walk with Him.

As you become aware of the kingdom, you will begin to have kingdom sightings. It will show up in your home and at your work; while driving, talking, and sleeping. Simply embrace it. And before your know it, the King and His kingdom will have reformed you into a kingdom expression. It is in this reformed place that we are equipped to impart. We must impart to our children a passion for the Holy Spirit and the kingdom.

Commitment

God plans on overcoming evil with good (Romans 12:21). To do this, there must be a commitment to doing good long-term. In the same chapter of Romans, Paul instructs us to bless those who persecute us (Romans 12:14). People are persecuted because they challenge a culture's values and traditions. As we challenge through love, service, humility, radical generosity, and obedience, we must understand that there will be persecution, and our response must be to bless those who do.

For sometime there has seemed to be two groups in the church. One clings to judgment, believing their role in the world is to remind it of its wickedness and death. But their screams never transform the dead. The other group, considered more liberal, simply opens up their arms and embraces the wickedness under the banner of mercy and grace. But their open arms do not produce transformation either. There must be a middle ground toiled by mercy and truth that empowers people by grace to see transformation. We must become more intentional in discriminating what is right and wrong and more deliberate in showing mercy. This balance, committed to the long-term, will overcome evil.

Commitment is an issue of the heart that lies past emotions and feelings in the core of a person. Commitment expresses itself through the virtue of diligence. Commitment is not excessive apathy that does not want to move and remains still; nor is it the inability to make a decision. This laziness is the opposite of commitment and diligence. With commitment comes a freedom. Life is lived more freely` when you have fully committed yourself to one option. Commitment cuts down on the options and frees a person to think about more productive ideas. The proverb says, "Commit your works to the Lord, and your thoughts will be established" (16:3). "The irony of commitment is that it's deeply liberating—in work, in play, in love. The act frees you from the tyranny of your internal critic, from the fear that likes to dress itself up and parade around as rational hesitation. "To commit is to remove your head as the barrier to your life" (Anne Morriss). We must live committed to a person; the Holy Spirit, and in doing so, we live committed to the values of the kingdom. We must choose to commit ourselves to holding and expressing the values of the kingdom in every area of our lives. As we live out the values of the kingdom we live from the heart, because your treasure is where you heart is. So, we must commit to diligently living out the values of the kingdom as we live following the guide!

We Are the Plan

In the fullness of time, God sent forth one man completely reliant on Him with the gospel of the kingdom. When God was ready to offer a solution to the world's corruption, He sent His Son. I do not think He has a back-up plan. I believe that when God wants to bring solutions to the world's problems, He sends His adopted sons to release the only begotten Son. This is His plan. God tends to hide things in the most unlikely places. He has hidden the solutions to poverty, civil rights, AIDS, the economy, abortion, and all the world's problems in the last place most people would look- us! So, that He might receive all the glory.

We must learn that it is the presence of God (Holy Spirit) that qualifies us to do the impossible. Like Gideon, Moses, Joshua, David, and Jesus we must value the presence of God more than anything else in the world. The Bible says that the dove remained on Jesus. We must value the dove on our shoulders more than anything the world has to offer. This is seeking first the kingdom.

Father God is transforming His sons and daughters. He is "kingdomizing" them, and once they are, He plans on sending them out, receiving His love and giving it away. In doing so, He will be reconciling the scattered orphans of the earth back to Himself and taking the kingdoms of the earth and bringing them under the His reign (Revelation 11:15). So, let me conclude with a call from God to you, calling you to your kingdom destiny:

Arise, shine; for your light has come! And the glory of the Lord is risen upon you. For behold, the darkness shall cover the earth, and deep darkness the people; But the Lord will arise over you, and His glory will be seen upon you.

Isaiah 60:1–2

REFERENCES

Crosswalk. Copyright 2007. "http://bible1.crosswalk.com/"http://bible1.crosswalk.com/

New King James Version. Thomas Nelson Publishers, 1997.

Vine, W.E. Vine's Expository Dictionary, Thomas Nelson Publishers; Nashville, 1996

Wuest, Kenneth. Word studies in the Greek New Testament. Esrdmans Publishing Company; Grand Rapids, Michigan, 1973

NKJV Study Bible—all scripture references taken from NKJV unless otherwise noted.

APPENDIX A:

Therefore I also, after I heard of your faith in the Lord Jesus and your love for all the saints, do not cease to give thanks for you, making mention of you in my prayers: that the God of our Lord Jesus Christ, the Father of glory, may give to you the spirit of wisdom and revelation in the knowledge of Him, that the eyes of your understanding be enlightened; that you may know what is the hope of His calling, what are the riches of the glory of His inheritance in the saints, and what is the exceeding greatness of His power towards us who believe, according to the working of His mighty power which He worked in Christ when He raised Him from the dead and seated Him at His right hand in the heavenly places, far above all principality and power and might and dominion, and every name that is named, not only in this age but also in that which is to come. And He put all things under His feet, and gave Him to be head over all things to the church, which is His body, the fullness of Him who fills all in all.

Ephesians 1:15–23

Chosen, Redeemed, Sealed

The passage of Scripture that I want to dissect is Ephesians 1:15–23. Verse 15 starts with 'therefore,' which is actually referring to the beginning of the chapter in verses 3–14. These verses teach that the believer is chosen by God (3–6), redeemed by the Son (7–12), and then sealed by the Holy Spirit (13–14).

CHOSEN BY GOD

I believe that God has chosen and predetermined that anyone in Christ will be made holy, blameless, and adopted as His sons. God has not predetermined who will live eternally in heaven and who will live eternally in hell. He has predetermined the rewards for those who believe in Christ. He foreknows who will believe in Him but allows them to choose. For example, if life were a race (hypothetically), God predetermines the reward for those who run, but not who decides to run.

REDEEMED BY THE SON

The "mystery" of God's will in verse 9 has been disclosed; it is CHRIST! The world has been groaning and searching for something more, something greater, something purposeful, and God in His own time has sent us Jesus. In Christ is the forgiveness of sins, freedom from bondage, and grace abundant. We can never achieve these things in our own power, but we can receive them by faith alone.

SEALED BY THE HOLY SPIRIT

There are actually three basic implications and uses of the Greek word for "sealed," *sphragizo:*

(1) a document would be sealed when a transaction was final,

(2) a seal was placed on animals and other things projecting ownership, and

(3) a seal was placed on something to keep it secure while traveling (Wuest).

In the same way, the Holy Spirit is our seal that a transaction has been made and Christ has purchased us, becoming our Lord or Master. He has secured our salvation in the sense that we cannot sin in our spirits but only in our soul and body, thus we make the journey through this life safely. So we can see that Ephesians 1:15–23 is prefaced with a reminder to the believer that they are chosen, redeemed, and sealed. Paul, however, knows that God has more for the saints that He wants to show them. Let's look.

The Breakdown

> Therefore I also, after I heard of your faith in the Lord Jesus and your love for all the saints, do not cease to give thanks for you, making mention of you in my prayers…

Notice that Paul places the invisible with the invisible (faith and the Lord) and the visible with the visible (love and the saints). Faith cannot be seen by the physical eye, nor have most believers seen Jesus physically. Love as an action can be seen, just as the saints can be seen. Paul is showing us that the fruit of faith in Jesus is love for the saints. One may say they have faith, but let them prove it by love for the saints. This is the result of life. Remember the life that Christ brings is first a life of love.

This is important for my generation: the "postmoderns" of the world. Many of our younger followers of Christ have given up on the church. By focusing on what she does wrong instead of the husband she is destined to marry, many become bitter at the very object of Christ's affections. I once held some false beliefs that allowed me, without any conviction, to think that I was following Christ while being full of bitterness at his body! If I am following Christ, His heart will become mine and His heart is crazy, head over heals in love with His bride to be! In spite of all her faults and blemishes that we may see, He sees through them and loves what He sees.

Paul is moved to thanking God because of the witness of the love that the Ephesians have for each other, which tells me that God's working in you ought to bring thankfulness to me. Paul has a kingdom view. The growth and maturity of the saints causes him to rejoice. Imagine if we as believers would rejoice over other people's personal growth in the kingdom whether or not they were a part of our church or denomination. If a Christian lives with a kingdom mindset, godly growth in any person is growth to the kingdom and should be celebrated. There should be no jealousy and no competition, only thankfulness and rejoicing.

"... that the God of our Lord Jesus Christ, the Father of glory ..."

Paul uses a great description to identify who God is. When God showed Himself to Moses, He used a relationship He had with others to describe Himself. "I am the God of Abraham, Isaac, and Jacob" (Exodus 3:6). Moses could relate to God by remembering how God related to Abraham, Isaac, and Jacob. Paul is doing the same by focusing our thoughts on remembering who our God is.

Before he asks God to give the church the "spirit of wisdom and revelation" he reminds them that God is a giver. Their God and ours is the God of our Lord Jesus. Our God did not withhold from us the greatest gift ever to be given, Jesus Christ. Paul is stirring the faith of the saints in Ephesus by reminding them that our God is good, and "No good thing will He withhold from those who walk uprightly" (Psalm 84:11b). If our God gave the most glorious and precious gift He could give, which is Christ, why would He withhold a lesser gift? Remember as Paul continues that we are not presenting our requests to a God whose response we cannot be sure of, or a God who is not willing, but to the God who has proven to be more than willing to give, even Himself!

"... may give you the spirit of wisdom and revelation ..."

Here, in verse 17, Paul requests of God to give you the spirit of wisdom and revelation. There is only one Holy Spirit (Ephesians 4:4), and Paul is asking the Spirit to manifest Himself through wisdom and revelation. For example, someone with a spirit (or gift) of discernment does not have a separate spirit from the Holy Spirit, but is allowing the Holy Spirit to manifest Himself through discernment. This is consistent with Paul's writing in 1 Corinthians 2:10, "But God has revealed them to us through His Spirit," and 1 Corinthians 2:14, "but the natural man does not receive the things of the Spirit of God, for they are foolishness to him; nor can he know them, because they are spiritually discerned." Notice that the Spirit brings revelation.

The word "revelation" used in verse 17 is the Greek word *apokalupsis*. According to Vine's Expository dictionary, this word could mean a number of things:

(a) an uncovering,

(b) the drawing away by Christ of the veil of darkness,

(c) the communication of knowledge of God to the soul, or

(d) an expression of the mind of God for the instruction of the church.

Furthermore, according to the New American Standard Strong's Expository Dictionary, this feminine noun could also mean:

(a) manifestation,

(b) appearance, or

(c) to lay bare or make naked.

Paul is asking God to uncover or make naked the truth in the knowledge of Himself. This knowledge cannot be attained by intellectual exercise but only by the Holy Spirit.

" ... in the knowledge of Him ..."

"In Him" is an important part of this verse and is largely forgotten in many interpretations: the Spirit will bring wisdom and revelation, but this wisdom and revelation will be in terms of Jesus. So, whatever Paul is about to request of God to show the saints will be in terms of Jesus of Nazareth. Jesus is truth and any revelation of truth will be a revelation of Jesus or because of Jesus.

" ... the eyes of your understanding being enlightened ..."

Paul focuses on the "eyes of the understanding" or heart. (Although the New King James translation renders the Greek word *kardia* as "understanding," this word is most commonly translated as "heart.") *Kardia* means the center and seat of spiritual life—the soul; the fountain and seat of the thoughts, passions, desires, appetites, affections, purposes, endeavors of the understanding, the faculty and seat of the intelligence of the will and character (crosswalk.com). The heart is different than the mind. It is not simply thoughts that would take place in the mind but the "fountain" or the "why" of the thoughts—the thing that motivates the thoughts, the thing that controls the will.

The word "enlightened" in this passage is a perfect participle—it is a past, complete act that has present results (Wuest). Paul is praying that a concrete act of the Holy Spirit be done in the human spirits of these saints, that they will have the spiritual capacity to understand and receive lasting benefits. Paul is about to pray for the eyes of the believer's heart to be enlightened to three truths.

" ... that you my know what is the hope of His calling ... "

"Hope" in this verse is not the object to be obtained but the attitude of the believer's mind and heart, their confident assurance. "His calling" does not mean a calling that God is called to, but a calling of which He is the author. So, in English, Paul is praying for the Spirit of God to enlighten, or uncover, truth to the saints, which will cause the saints to experientially know God's calling, which will function as the object of their hope (confident assurance).

The application of this truth is important. Our calling comes from a revelatory knowledge of Christ, which means Christ at some level is the high calling of every believer. When I think of Jesus being the standard of the high calling that I am to attain, I do not feel hope but disappointment. However, I feel disappointment because I know that I cannot, in and of myself, obtain this call. The good news is that if the revelation comes by the Spirit (which is the only way it comes), then that revelation must also be worked out by the power of the Spirit. This revelation brings hope because God wants the believer to look like Jesus, and no spoken word of God comes void of the power needed to perform it.

This harmonizes with what Paul says in Romans 8:29, "For whom He (God) foreknew, He also predestined to be conformed to the image of His Son, that He (Jesus) might be the firstborn among many brethren." God predetermined that those who would believe in Christ, those He foreknew (not picked), would be conformed into the image of Jesus. *God wants us to look like Jesus,* and no matter what, we will eventually look like Him. However, there is more of His image to be conformed to now than one may think. This is why John states, "…because as He is, so are we in this world" (1 John 4:17). If this is true, then we must ask ourselves, what was Jesus here for? 1 John 3:8b says, "…For this purpose the Son of God was manifested, that He might destroy the works of the devil." Everything Jesus did—preach, teach, heal, die, rise—was to destroy the works of the devil.

This is our calling: to co-labor with the King of Kings, destroying the works of the devil. Jesus conquered sin and death, and rendered the devil powerless on the cross and in the resurrection. Our calling is to enforce the victory of the cross by binding the devil where he is still working and loosing the kingdom of God.

Jesus only mentions the "church" twice in context, Matthew 16 and 18, and both times He mentions the church the same verse follows. "…whatever you bind on earth will be bound in heaven, and whatever you loose on earth will be loosed in heaven" (Matthew 16:19 ; 18:18). I think this verse is better translated "whatever you bind on earth shall have been bound in heaven." The point has been made that a person cannot bind something in time and it be bound in eternity. I am to bind what is already bound in heaven. Heaven is my model. "On earth as it is in heaven."

I believe this is what Paul meant in Ephesians 3:10, "His (God's) intent (purpose or will) was that now through the church, (the redeemed or believing ones) the manifold wisdom of God should be made known to the rulers and authorities in the heavenly realms (in heavenly realms means either angels or demons), according to His eternal purpose which He accomplished in Christ Jesus our Lord." (NIV)

" ... what are the riches of the glory of His inheritance in the saints ..."

"In the saints" is the location of this inheritance. That is, the sphere of the saints is definitive of the word "inheritance" (Wuest). Paul is saying that the saints are God's inheritance, and Paul is praying that the saints might know how precious they are in God's eyes as His inheritance. Not only do the saints receive a good inheritance, but God wants us to know He views the redeemed as a beautiful inheritance. He is glorified in His saints, and His glory is valuable.

God is madly in love with us. I once heard a televangelist say, "There is something about you that turns God on." Many people said amen, but I was shocked! What if my attractiveness to Him is my hair and I go bald? Or my strength and I grow weak? Or my flat stomach (which has already escaped)? I do not need to know there is something about me that makes me likable or appealing to God, but I need to know that there is something about God that will keep Him in love with me! And there is: God is love.

God will never wake up on the wrong side of the bed with high blood pressure and be a grouch. This is love, not that I loved God but that He first loved me! Even when I was an enemy to Him, He loved me. Allow this truth to free you. God has seen and heard all that you have done, will do, or have thought of doing. He has seen your heart with all its crooked motives—both the past and the future—and the verdict remains the same: He loves you.

One way of determining if your heart has been enlightened to how precious an inheritance you are to him is how deeply you love Him. However, many of us struggle to love him back. On one occasion, I was fasting and praying for God to teach me or make me love Him more. (I know, it sounds legalistic when I write it down.) During this time, a group from our church went over to a member's house to share dinner and fellowship. I watched as a young mother held her baby. The little girl had the "baby glaze" on her face, and then her mother started smiling at her and making those goofy baby noises. The baby began to smile, and as I watched, the Lord spoke into my spirit. He said, "I will love you into loving me, the way a mother smiles a baby into smiling." If you are not loving God the way you desire, the secret is not to try harder, but to receive His love more. When I can realize how much He loves me and how precious I am in His sight, then my heart will be moved to love Him in return, and it will not be by trying, but by receiving and releasing it back.

" ... and what is the exceeding greatness of His power toward us who believe, according to the working of His mighty power ..."

"Exceedingly" denotes a power that is more than enough. The power made available through Jesus exceeds anything the saints might face. This power exceeds our addictions, exceeds our rebellion, exceeds the hatred, the bitterness, the evil or darkness in this present age. "Toward us" is better translated "us-ward" and "who believe" is better translated "believing ones." This power is not just available to be tapped into; it is actually for us. If God's power was an awesome river, He did not think to Himself, "all right I guess you guys can get a little wet." No, He actually gives the believing ones a right to swim!

Then Paul gives an example of this power available to the saints in verse 20. It is not merely related to the power that raised Christ from the dead—it is that same power that raised Him from the dead. Think about the implications of what Paul is saying. Two thousand years ago a lifeless corpse lay in a cave carved out of the rocks used as a tomb. After three days of being dead, the Spirit of Power caused the life and spirit of Christ to re-enter that body and come alive. Now this same power, not one like it but *the same exact power,* flows through the spirit of every believer. If you are a believer, then as you read this, that power is in you!

Notice that Paul neither writes nor implies that the saints have to go earn this power. It comes when the Spirit of the Almighty God awakens the saints to this power that is in Christ and towards us. The power of God is not a lake that needs construction in order to flow to us, but a river that runs right for the redeemed. This river must be dammed in order to be rendered ineffective. This is why new converts, who have been taught neither good nor bad theology, can function in the gifts and power of the Holy Spirit. The same power that raised Christ from the dead is not achieved; it is in Christ, and when a sinner is placed "in Christ," the power that raised Christ from the dead is in the new believer.

" ... which He worked in Christ when He raised Him from the dead ..."

This power is the same power that raised Christ from the dead (seems a bit redundant but hang with me). This means that this power has the ability to take something spiritual and make it manifest in the physical. Jesus's corpse was wrapped and put into the tomb, but Jesus's spirit was not dead. This power is what took the spirit of Christ (which is spiritual) and the lifeless corpse of Christ (which is physical) and caused a collision and the spiritual manifested in the physical, resulting in life.

Why waste a paragraph on this point? Because if I have been given all I need for life and godliness, where is it located? I am blessed with every spiritual blessing but it is in heavenly places. I have a calling that is great and all the necessities for obtaining and walking in my calling are in the spiritual realm. So, I need a power that can take something in the spiritual realm and cause a manifestation in the physical realm!

To take it one step further, God has already paid for every man's salvation. When one calls on the name of the Lord to be ransomed, Jesus does not go back and die. So where is this salvation waiting?; the Spiritual realm. If Jesus in fact paid for our healing, because by his stripes we are healed (Isaiah 53:4–6), then where is the healing waiting? If God wants His will to be done on earth (physical) as it is in heaven (spiritual), then we need this power that can cause the spiritual to invade the physical.

> **" ... and seated Him at His right hand in the heavenly places, far above all principality and power and might and dominion, and every name that is named, not only in this age but also in that which is to come. And He put all things under His feet, and gave Him to be head over all things in the church ..."**

"Far above" is *huperano,* which literally means "over above" (Wuest). "Principality" is the translation of *arche,* and literally means "first ones, or leader" (Vine's). *Exousia* is translated power, "delegated authority" (Wuest). "Dominion" is *kuriotes,* which is "lordship." "And every name" means literally every name. The word "placed" in verse 22 is the Greek word *hupotasso,* which is a military term meaning "to put in subjection under one" (Wuest). The word translated by the NIV as "appointed" is actually the same word as "gave," as in a gift. God placed Jesus over and above all authorities whether governmental, religious, or in the workplace. God made every name subject to Jesus including arthritis, Alzheimer's, cancer, glaucoma, recession, and the like. Jesus has all dominion, even over depression, hatred, bitterness, suicide, and any other demonic influence. God made all things subject to Jesus and then gave Jesus as a gift to the church to be her head. Receive this gift, this wonderful gift!

" ... which is His body, the fullness of Him who fills all in all."

"Which is His body" denotes a close bond. It is not just King and servants, but intimate and lively. The Church is not merely an institution ruled by Him as President, or a kingdom in which He is the Supreme Authority, but a society which is in vital connection with Him, having the source of its life in Him, sustained and directed by His power, and the church is also the instrument by which He works. Yes, He is King and Supreme Authority, but His relationship with His bride is far more intimate than that. Paul, by way of illustration, is reinforcing the first of these three awakenings. As His body, the church is the instrument by which Jesus will work. So, if Jesus is going to preach, whose voice will He use? If He is going to heal the sick, whose hands will He use? If He is going to raise the dead, who will He use to bring life? If He is going to care for the poor, whose heart will He fill with compassion? If He is going to bless a businessman in such a way that this man will effect the nations, which businessman will He choose? The redeemed! There is no plan B; the church will represent Jesus regardless of her setbacks and failures!

In the context of verses 22 and 23, one should come to the conclusion that if all things are under Christ's feet, and the church is

His body, then all things are under the church's feet. This is the revelation to which our hearts must be enlightened—we are already, in Christ, more than conquerors. Paul must have wanted to ask the question, "Why, when you are called and commanded to be like Jesus and are God's glorious inheritance, and have the same power that raised Christ from the dead inside of you, do you live at such a low level of victory?" Maybe we should stop and ask ourselves the same questions.

What's the Problem?

The saints in Ephesus had not received a revelation of these truths we are discussing, or if they had the devil snatched it away, or they stumbled under persecution, or the cares of this world choked out the revelation (Matthew 13:19–23), or they did not remain abiding in this revelation (John 8:31). Paul is praying for an awakening of their spirits, an enlightening in their hearts, a revelation of themselves in Jesus Christ.

How can Christians have and be all the things God says they are and not know it? How can I be something and not live like it?

A People Divided

A person is divided into three parts: spirit, soul, and body (1 Thessalonians 5:23). In the fall of man, man experienced three deaths. Adam died in his spirit. The Bibles records the Lord saying, "…in the day that you eat of it you shall surely die" (Genesis 2:17). Notice the language "in the day." Obviously, the day Adam ate of the fruit he did not die physically; he lived for hundreds of years. Adam died spiritually immediately, then He died progressively in his soul. His mind, emotions, will, and the intentions of his heart grew in death (the Bible describes men in the day of Noah: "…every intent of the thoughts of his heart was only evil continually…" (Genesis 6:5), until Adam eventually died physically.

Look at the reverse. When a person is saved, are they saved the moment they call on the name of the Lord? Yes, but where? In their spirits. Spiritually they become alive, then their soul is progressively redeemed as they renew their mind, and finally a Christian will receive a new body in heaven; three parts, three deaths, three salvations.

All three revelations that Paul prayed for the saints to be enlightened to are located in the Christian's spirit. There must be an enlightenment or an awakening to the "heart" or "understanding" of man for these truths to become tangible or manifest. This does not necessarily mean that there is full understanding or comprehension, but a realization of what Christ has accomplished for us to walk in. I do not have to completely understand how my car operates to benefit from it; however, I do need to know that I have the keys and the license to drive the car.

The Pipe

…while we do not look at the things which are seen, but at the things which are not seen. For the things which are seen are temporary, but the things which are not seen are eternal.

2 Corinthians 4:18

Picture a pipe. One end of this pipe is connected to an endless supply of water and the other is an outlet from which the water is to be flowing. However, it is not. The reason is that in the middle of this pipe, between the endless supply and the outlet, is a closed pipe valve. All that is needed is a turn of the valve and, voilà! What was once unseen becomes visible. Similarly, this endless water supply represents the Holy Spirit in your spirit (a river of living water), the outlet is where the water becomes tangible or beneficial, and the pipe valve is the soul (mind, will and emotions).

Turning the Valve

Our souls must be trained to operate out of truth. When I walk in defeat, depression, anxiety, or bitterness, I am not thinking as the Bible is telling me I should. When I walk around feeling powerless, purposeless, and that I am of no value to anyone, I am not thinking according to truth. Remember our core values are the lens through which we view reality.

Christians have lived with an unrenewed mind for so long that it seems drastic or extreme to actually believe what the Bible says! However, this is how God's declaration of who I am comes to life. When I renew my mind, I am transformed; when transformed, I prove (make tangible) the will of God (Romans 12:2). "Now we have received, not the spirit of the world, but the Spirit who is from God, that we might know the things that have been freely given to us by God" (1 Corinthians 2:12). God has accomplished so much in the resurrection of Jesus Christ that He has to send His presence (Spirit) to guide us, that we may know what He has freely given us. Incredible!

This is a simple analogy that has helped me. For the redeemed person the Bible teaches that their spirit has been made the righteousness of Christ. However, they have an unrenewed soul (mind, will, and emotions) and body. The body has it's own cravings. The spirit has its own cravings. The saint's spirit longs to walk with God. If you chose to join your soul with your spirit you will walk out the Christian life. If you join your soul with your body you will satisfy the desires of the flesh. A Christian cannot satisfy the flesh and enjoy it for the long haul. God has made us free (Galatians 5:1) to choose which we will join our soul to.

This means we cannot access the benefits of the cross and resurrection without the Holy Spirit. To obtain what God has purchased for us we need God (the Holy Spirit) to show us what we have access to by faith—and even our faith is a gift from God! It is Christ, working through Christ, to reveal Christ to us, in order for us to manifest Christ. He truly is our all in all!

listen|imagine|view|experience

AUDIO BOOK DOWNLOAD INCLUDED WITH THIS BOOK!

In your hands you hold a complete digital entertainment package. In addition to the paper version, you receive a free download of the audio version of this book. Simply use the code listed below when visiting our website. Once downloaded to your computer, you can listen to the book through your computer s speakers, burn it to an audio CD or save the file to your portable music device (such as Apple s popular iPod) and listen on the go!

How to get your free audio book digital download:

1. Visit www.tatepublishing.com and click on the e|LIVE logo on the home page.
2. Enter the following coupon code:
   f0c0-8b78-d930-490a-4150-c381-cec1-0942
3. Download the audio book from your e|LIVE digital locker and begin enjoying your new digital entertainment package today!